At Issue

Do Children Have Rights?

Other Books in the At Issue Series:

At Issue

Do Children Have Rights?

Christine Watkins, Book Editor

GREENHAVEN PRESS
A part of Gale, Cengage Learning

GALE
CENGAGE Learning·

Detroit • New York • San Francisco • New Haven, Conn • Waterville, Maine • London

GALE
CENGAGE Learning™

Christine Nasso, *Publisher*
Elizabeth Des Chenes, *Managing Editor*

© 2011 Greenhaven Press, a part of Gale, Cengage Learning.

Gale and Greenhaven Press are registered trademarks used herein under license.

For more information, contact:
Greenhaven Press
27500 Drake Rd.
Farmington Hills, MI 48331-3535
Or you can visit our Internet site at gale.cengage.com

For product information and technology assistance, contact us at

Gale Customer Support, 1-800-877-4253
For permission to use material from this text or product, submit all requests online at www.cengage.com/permissions.

Further permissions questions can be e-mailed to permissionrequest@cengage.com.

Articles in Greenhaven Press anthologies are often edited for length to meet page requirements. In addition, original titles of these works are changed to clearly present the main thesis and to explicitly indicate the author's opinion. Every effort is made to ensure that Greenhaven Press accurately reflects the original intent of the authors. Every effort has been made to trace the owners of copyrighted material.

Cover image © Images.com/Corbis.

LIBRARY OF CONGRESS CATALOGING-IN-PUBLICATION DATA

Do children have rights? / Christine Watkins, book editor.
    p. cm. -- (At issue)
  Includes bibliographical references and index.
  ISBN 978-0-7377-4876-5 (hardcover) -- ISBN 978-0-7377-4877-2 (pbk.)
  1. Children's rights--Juvenile literature. 2. Children--Legal status, laws, etc.--Juvenile literature. 3. Child labor--Juvenile literature. 4. Sex instruction for children--Juvenile literature. I. Watkins, Christine, 1951-
  HQ789.D622 2010
  323.3'52--dc22

                       2010021987

Printed in the United States of America
1 2 3 4 5 6 7 14 13 12 11 10

Contents

Introduction

More than half a million children—some under the age of ten—have been recruited into armed forces in more than eighty-five countries worldwide, according to the Coalition to Stop the Use of Child Soldiers. And girls are not excluded; they are recruited as active combatants, in addition to roles as prostitutes, as sex slaves, and as "wives" for other combatants. Children are targeted because of their inexperience and vulnerability, making them more easily indoctrinated; if they resist, drugs are often used to break down any psychological barriers. Once recruited, these children can be subjected to brutal initiation rituals in which they are forced to kill or injure members of their own families, and youngsters are beaten or killed if they try to escape.

> When I was abducted in 2003, we had no food for three days. We lived only on water. . . . They [the rebels] told us to decide among ourselves who should be eaten. At first we thought it was a joke until they decided themselves on a certain girl whom they slaughtered and cut into pieces. Then they told us to cook the pieces. When it was ready, the rebels forced us to eat the cooked girl. After that we were told to kill an old man who was helpless. After a week, the rebels brought us to Amaseniko camp [in Amuria district in eastern Uganda], where we had been abducted, and told us to burn houses. I was told to kill my grandfather. When I tried to refuse, the rebels beat me hard until I accepted to kill him using heavy stones. Then we went ahead to kill two more people we came across.

This was recounted by a thirteen-year-old girl to researchers for the February 2008 report "Returning Home—Children's Perspectives on Reintegration: A Case Study of Children Abducted by the Lord's Resistance Army in Teso, Eastern Uganda," by the Coalition to Stop the Use of Child Soldiers.

Her story is just one of many. According to the United Nations Children's Fund (UNICEF), this "illegal and morally reprehensible practice" of using children as soldiers continues in many armed conflicts around the world, despite efforts by the international community to end it.

Such efforts to end the use of child soldiers include the Optional Protocol to the Convention on the Rights of the Child on the Involvement of Children in Armed Conflict set forth by the United Nations in 2002. It outlaws the recruitment or participation of anyone under the age of eighteen in insurgency groups, rebel forces, or government and nongovernment armed forces "under any circumstances." Almost two thirds of the world's states have ratified the Optional Protocol, and others prohibit the use of child soldiers through their own national or state laws. Additionally, the International Criminal Court now has the jurisdiction to investigate the recruitment and use of child soldiers, and new mechanisms to monitor and report abuses against children have been put in place, as well as initiatives to build awareness among armed groups about children's rights. And for children who have escaped or been released from fighting forces, programs for disarmament, demobilization, and reintegration (DDR) have been established to assist them in returning and reintegrating into their families and communities.

These DDR programs represent a significant challenge in providing former child soldiers the special care and support needed while trying to reintegrate into society. Although it is widely accepted that children who have been illegally recruited by fighting forces should be treated as victims, they have in many cases been charged and detained as war criminals. In other situations, thousands of former child soldiers—especially girls—are afraid of being stigmatized by members of their communities and, therefore, do not register for DDR programs. Even when children do register for DDR programs, lack of funding, poor planning, and mismanagement often undermine the long-term psychosocial support, vocational training, and education these children need to successfully return to civilian life. And so, while some progress has been made in helping child soldiers, much more needs to be done, particularly with regard to preventing child involvement in the first place. According to the "Child Soldiers Global Report 2008" from the Coalition to Stop the Use of Child Soldiers:

> The overall picture is one of armed groups that have ignored international law and standards, that renege on commitments, are resistant to pressure and persuasion, or have so far proved to be beyond the reach of efforts to end the involvement of children in conflict and political violence.

According to the United Nations Convention on the Rights of the Child, every child has the right to survival; the right to develop to the fullest; the right to be protected from harmful influences, abuse, and exploitation; and the right to participate in family, culture, and social life. As soldiers, children are denied these rights. They are robbed of their childhood and exposed to terrible danger and to psychological, emotional, and physical suffering. The authors in *At Issue: Do Children Have Rights?* discuss other legal, ethical, developmental, and emotional issues concerning the rights children do or do not have.

1

Children Do Have Rights

United Nations Children's Fund (UNICEF)

The United Nations Children's Fund (UNICEF) is a multinational organization that provides health care, clean water, improved nutrition, and education to millions of children worldwide.

On November 20, 1989, world leaders came together in the United Nations General Assembly to adopt the Convention on the Rights of the Child. As the most-ratified human rights treaty in history, the convention articulates that children have the right to survive and develop; to be protected from violence, abuse, and exploitation; and for their views to be respected. It should be especially noted that children have the right to participate in decisions that affect their lives; this principle is less understood and championed than the basic rights of survival and protection. Experts, policy makers, and youth organizations are becoming increasingly aware that involving young people in decision-making processes enhances their development, resilience, and ability to protect themselves from abuse and exploitation.

On 20 November 2009, the global community celebrates the 20th anniversary of the adoption by the United Nations General Assembly of the Convention on the Rights of the Child. This unique document outlines universal standards for the care, treatment and protection of all individuals below age 18. It is the most widely endorsed human rights treaty in history, currently ratified by 193 States parties.

United Nations Children's Fund, "The State of the World's Children, Special Edition," New York: UNICEF, 2009. Copyright © 2009 UNICEF. Reproduced by permission.

During the past two decades, the Convention has transformed the way children are viewed and treated throughout the world. It has exerted a pervasive and profound influence on national and international legislation, policy and programmes, public and private institutions, families, communities and individuals. And it has supported marked advances in survival, development, protection and participation across the world.

Despite the numerous challenges that remain in realizing children's rights, the Convention offers a vision of a world in which all children survive and develop, and are protected, respected and encouraged to participate in the decisions that affect them. This vision promotes a world of peace, tolerance, equity, respect for human rights and shared responsibility—in short, a world fit for children.

It is imperative to protect childhood as a period that is separate from adulthood.

The Convention on the Rights of the Child

The Convention on the Rights of the Child (henceforth referred to as 'the Convention') was adopted by the UN General Assembly on 20 November 1989 and entered into force on 2 September 1990. It is the most comprehensive human rights treaty and legal instrument for the promotion and protection of children's rights. Although there are provisions protecting child rights in other international human rights instruments, the Convention is the first to articulate the entire complement of rights relevant to children—economic, social, cultural, civil and political. It was also the first international instrument to explicitly recognize children as social actors and active holders of their own rights.

Under the provisions of the treaty, States parties are legally obliged to fulfil the rights of every child. The Convention comprises 54 articles and is based on four core principles: non-discrimination; best interests of the child; the right to life, survival and development; and respect for the views of children. Its broad scope and the importance it places on the agency of the child make it timelessly relevant to all actions that intend to promote, protect and fulfil children's rights.

The Convention is a powerful addition to the international human rights framework. Although it has been in existence for only two decades, it has achieved near-universal acceptance, having been ratified by 193 countries by 2009, with only two outstanding: Somalia and the United States, both of which have indicated their support by signing the treaty. The influence of the Convention and its Optional Protocols is already pervasive across continents and regions, countries and communities, and it will clearly remain the children's Magna Carta for decades—possibly even centuries—to come.

The Convention has significantly reaffirmed and enriched human rights. It reaffirms by applying many of the core principles of earlier international human rights instruments, such as universality and non-discrimination, directly to children. It enriches by consolidating and amplifying the provisions that are included in other human rights instruments, specifying the responsibilities and duties of States parties towards children. It incorporates rights for children that were not widely articulated—notably the right to participation—and stipulates that the best interests of the child should be a primary consideration in all actions towards them. It stresses that accountability for child rights lies with the duty bearers, including States parties, families and guardians, who are entrusted with ensuring that children's rights are realized.

"Terms of Childhood"

The full significance of the Convention extends well beyond its legislative implications. It has also helped transform attitudes towards childhood. In effect, the Convention has set the *terms of childhood*, outlining the minimum standards for the treatment, care, survival, development, protection and participation that are due every individual under age 18. Its articles reinforce a common understanding among societies that to fulfil the rights of children it is imperative to protect childhood as a period that is separate from adulthood, to define a time in which children can grow, learn, play and develop.

Under the Convention, children are rights holders rather than objects of charity. Fulfilling these rights is no longer an option for States parties but an obligation that governments have pledged to meet. Equally important is the optimism, clarity and steadfastness that the Convention captures for the future—that one day all children will enjoy a childhood with full respect for their rights, their basic needs provided for, protected from violence, abuse, exploitation, neglect and discrimination, and empowered to participate meaningfully in all decisions that affect their lives.

In its preamble and throughout its articles the Convention underscores the fundamental role of the family in the growth and well-being of children, recognizing the crucial importance of a loving, harmonious and understanding family environment for the full development of children. It obliges States parties to provide the family with all the means necessary to realize its responsibilities. . . .

The Right to Be Heard

Participation is one of the guiding principles of the Convention on the Rights of the Child, yet it is arguably taken less seriously than the other key principles of universality, the best interests of the child, and survival and development. To some extent, child participation may be seen as more controversial, challenging or difficult to implement than measures supporting child survival, development and protection because it is based on presenting children as rights holders rather than as

13

recipients of charity. Also, there is less experience in this area among the child rights community than in survival, development and protection.

The Convention does not use the term 'participation' or explicitly state that children have a right to participate—except as a goal for children with disabilities (article 23). But it requires that their views be heard in relation to all matters that affect them and that their views be given due weight in accordance with their age and maturity (article 12). This right is part of a broader body of participation rights that children hold, starting with the right to freedom of expression (article 13), thought, conscience and religion (14), association (15), the right to privacy (16) and access to appropriate information (17) that provides the basis for the child's right to participate. The Convention refers to children's "evolving capacity" for decision-making—a revolutionary concept in international law—and this has profoundly influenced the practice of organizations working in the field during the past 20 years.

The right of children to participate is a fundamental component of respecting them as holders of their own rights. Being able to influence decisions that affect an individual is one of the defining characteristics of human rights principles. When it comes to designing opportunities for children to participate, conditions need to be adjusted in accordance with a child's age and maturity. They should not be pressured, constrained or influenced in ways that might prevent them from freely expressing their opinions or leave them feeling manipulated. Effective and meaningful participation depends on many factors, including the child's developing capabilities, the openness of parents and other adults to dialogue, and safe spaces within the family, community and society that allow such dialogue. It also depends on stakeholders being willing to take children's views into consideration. Much of the practice of child participation is based on children's right to expression in all matters affecting them—this has, to an increasing extent, guided legal processes in decisions relating to custody following divorce or disputes between parents and authorities over children taken into care.

The vast majority of public decisions affecting children are made, however, without considering the views of or involving children. Policies have traditionally focused on welfare, perceiving children as passive recipients of care and services, not public actors. In general, children are rarely able to exercise any influence over the resources allocated in their name. Much of the work of government and civil society is carried out without explicit recognition of children and young people. Interventions are implemented on behalf of children rather than with them.

Children are not generally seen as social and political actors. In most countries, individuals do not vote in national and local elections until they reach age 18. Children, therefore, often have no formal place at the decision-making table, and adult-controlled mechanisms are likely to be required for children's opinions to be represented. Children involved in political processes are often considered as technical actors who can provide useful information, rather than as citizens or political actors with rights to uphold and interests to defend.

Participation fosters the resilience of children and adolescents.

At conferences, adults may listen to children, but when it comes to the important decisions, children are often excluded. Youth parliaments may be little more than debating clubs where children learn about governance and politics. Some attempts at involving young people, moreover, are tokenistic— done more for the image of the adult organization bringing them together than for the benefit of the children themselves.

Participation and Empowerment

Children's participation has a vital role in empowering them in their own development. Through participation, girls and boys can learn vital life-skills and knowledge and take action to prevent and address abuse and exploitation. Participation initiatives are strengthened when children know and understand their rights. Consulting with children is critical to ensure that child survival, development and protection measures are adequate and appropriate.

There have been a growing number of initiatives in child participation since the Convention came into force in 1990. One highlight was the 2002 UN General Assembly Special Session on Children, an event that actively encouraged the participation of children in the principal decision-making body of the United Nations. More than 400 children from [more than] 150 countries took part in the three-day Children's Forum that culminated in a common statement from the participants reflecting their views.

The 2006 UN Secretary-General's Study on Violence against Children was the first United Nations study to consult with children and reflect and incorporate their views and recommendations. Children and adolescents participated in national, regional and international consultations, together with policymakers. To disseminate the findings of the study, child-friendly versions were created for a range of age groups. Children and adolescents were also strongly represented at the November 2008 Third World Congress against the Sexual Exploitation of Children and Adolescents in Rio de Janeiro (Brazil). . . .

In addition, child rights advocates are coming to recognize that participation by children and adolescents can play a vital part in protecting them from abuse, violence and exploitation. Participation fosters the resilience of children and adolescents and can enable them to become agents of change and to resist the processes that result in their abuse. It can also help them recover if they are abused, not least through sharing their experiences with their peers.

The theory and practice of children's participation is still in its infancy. But it has advanced significantly during the two decades since the Convention was adopted by the Member States of the United Nations. Moreover, the Convention has been a guiding force in encouraging greater child participation. Policymakers are becoming increasingly appreciative that involving young people in decision-making not only enhances children's development, protection and understanding of democracy, it improves outcomes for all. More children and young people are developing their capacity to participate and collaborate through youth organizations and networks to advocate for their rights.

2

Children's Rights Are Too Far Reaching

Patrick F. Fagan, William L. Saunders, and Michael A. Fragoso

Patrick F. Fagan is senior fellow and director of the Center for Research on Marriage and Religion at the Family Research Council (FRC), a Christian organization that promotes the traditional family unit. William L. Saunders is senior fellow and human rights counsel at the FRC. Michael A. Fragoso is a research assistant at the FRC.

The United Nations Convention on the Rights of the Child actually undermines the essence of family and parenthood by restricting the ability of parents to make decisions regarding how they parent their children. For example, United Nations committees urge children to challenge their parents in court regarding such time-honored parental responsibilities as supervision, discipline, moral and sexuality education, and even oversight of medical treatment. Most cultures and religions have respected the rights of parents to provide moral guidance for their children. The U.N. Committee on the Rights of the Child should not undermine parents' authority.

If the U.N. [United Nations] committees have their way, the freedom of parents to raise their own children, to shape their behaviors, and to safeguard their moral upbringing will be a relic of past centuries. That almost all cultures and religions have protected the time-honored role of parents in forming the character of children does not deter the U.N. from seeking changes in domestic laws to bypass parents on matters dealing with their children.

The U.N. Committee report to Belize recommends that the government set up legal mechanisms to help children challenge their parents.

The U.N. committees are urging states to give minor children:

• The right to privacy, even in the household;

• The right to professional counseling without parental consent or guidance;

• The full right to abortion and contraceptives, even when that would violate the parents' ethics and desires;

• The right to full freedom of expression at home and in school;

• The legal mechanisms to challenge in court their parents' authority in the home.

For example, the U.N. Committee on the Rights of the Child [CRC] recommends to the Japanese government that it "guarantee the child's right to privacy, especially in the family." Such a measure would establish legal and structural wedges between parents and their children in the home. Normally, when children rebel against their parents, society frowns. Yet the U.N. is attempting to put in place, in policy and law, structures that foster this type of rebellion.

Incites Children to Challenge Parental Role

Among the broad "rights" of children articulated in the CRC are freedom of expression; freedom to receive and impart all information and ideas, either orally, in writing, or in print, in the form of art, or through any other media of the child's choice; freedom of association; and freedom of peaceful assembly. This language could be interpreted to prohibit parents from legitimately limiting the associations and actions of their children, which can already be fraught with legal difficulties. Once these "rights" are embedded in domestic law, children could gain access to legal help from NGOs [nongovernmental organizations] or government agencies to challenge their parents in court.

Indeed, the U.N. committee report to Belize recommends that the government set up legal mechanisms to help children challenge their parents, including making an "independent child-friendly mechanism" accessible to children "to deal with complaints of violations of their rights and to provide remedies for such violations." In other words, the CRC committee is suggesting that the state create some entity *to supervise parents*, a structures that enables children in Belize to challenge their mother and father's parenting in court. Then the CRC committee goes even further: Its report asserts that it is "concerned that the law does not allow children, particularly adolescents, to seek medical or, legal counseling *without parental consent*, even when it is in the best interests of the child." This statement illustrates the committee's intent to undermine the authority of parents, especially those who hold traditional religious beliefs or who would disagree with the committee's radical interpretation of the CRC.

The U.N. committee's opposition to the freedom of parents to guide the moral education of their children is made clear in a rebuke directed at the United Kingdom in 1995. The committee stated that

> insufficient attention has been given to the right of the child to express his/her opinion, including in cases where parents in England and Wales have the possibility of withdrawing their children from parts of the sex education programs in

school. In this as in other decisions, including exclusion from school, the child is not systematically invited to express his/her opinion and those opinions may not be given due weight, as required under article 12 of the Convention.

The U.N. committee went even further in its recommendation to the Ethiopian government, urging it to change its laws so that "the limitation of the right to legal counsel of children be abolished as a matter of priority."

Consider the CRC committee's complaint to Austria: "Austrian Law and regulations do not provide a legal minimum age for medical counseling and treatment *without parental consent*." Austria, like all nations, has defined the age at which the child becomes legally independent of the parent. This effort by the U.N. committee to make states like Austria define a different age for medical counseling and treatment is targeted at removing parents' control over the moral formation of their children and the parameters of their children's sexual behavior.

The U.N. committee showed little awareness that Mali is among the poorest countries in the world, with 65 percent of its land area either desert or semi-desert. About 10 percent of the population is nomadic, and some 80 percent of the labor force is engaged in farming and fishing. Annual per capita GDP [gross domestic product] in Mali in 1998 was estimated to be $790. Yet the U.N. suggests that Mali allocate "adequate human and financial resources, to develop youth-friendly counseling, care and rehabilitation facilities for adolescents that would be *accessible without parental consent*, where this is in the best interests of the child."

Undermines Parental Influence Regarding Adolescent Sexual Behavior

The committee periodically issues "general comments" that are intended to flesh out the commitments inherent in the CRC treaty itself. The committee's General Comment No. 4

(2003) expounds upon "adolescent health and development in the context of the Convention on the Rights of the Child." This comment protects the right of children "to access appropriate information" regarding "family planning." It instructs states to allow minors to receive confidential medical care. They should have "access to appropriate information [regarding HIV/AIDS and STDs], regardless of their marital status and whether their parents or guardians consent." To that end the comment calls on states "to develop effective prevention . programmes, including efforts aimed at changing cultural views about adolescents' need for contraception and STD [sexually transmitted disease] prevention and addressing cultural and other taboos surrounding adolescent sexuality." To that end, states should "take measures to remove all barriers hindering the access of adolescents to information, preventative measures such as condoms, and care." It goes on to urge states "to develop and implement programmes that provide access to sexual and reproductive health services, including family planning, contraception and safe abortion services where abortion is not against the law . . ."

The broader agenda will weaken the freedom and authority of parents to direct the moral education and attitudes of their children.

General Comment No. 4 also unilaterally expands the purview of the CRC's anti-discrimination clause (Article 2), which states that minors enjoy the rights of the treaty "without discrimination . . . with regard to 'race, colour, sex, language, religion, political or other opinion, national, ethnic or social origin, property, disability, birth or other status.'" The committee expands this list of protected classes to include "adolescents' sexual orientation." The established frameworks of anti-discrimination architecture in U.N. treaties lack sexual orientation as a protected class, as no binding U.N. treaty mentions "sexual orientation." Thus, for the committee to act as if it does is mere liberal activism.

Restricts Parental Ability to Discipline Children

CRC's interpretative committee is also embroiled in efforts to outlaw spanking by parents. The committee, in 2006, issued General Comment No. 8, "The right of the child to protection from corporal punishment and other cruel or degrading forms of punishment," which purports to clarify articles 19, 28, and 37 of CRC. The comment deals with *any* physical punishment, "however light," and makes no distinction between disciplinary spanking and serious physical abuse, ranging from whipping, to kicking, to biting (paragraph 11). As such, it calls for states to ban all physical punishment of children through criminal law—the object being for the law to treat spanking as it would the battery of an adult. Furthermore, the comment instructs countries to undertake vast educational campaigns to "raise awareness" about the right of children not to be spanked. State parties are required to submit data on their progress toward eliminating "corporal punishment" during their periodic reviews: "The Committee also encourages United Nations agencies, national human rights institutions, NGOs and other competent bodies to provide it with relevant information on the legal status and prevalence of corporal punishment and progress towards its elimination."

The United States is not a state party to CRC, and yet anti-spanking activists have used these pronouncements from the CRC committee to argue that "consensus is growing in the international community that physical punishment of children violates international human rights law. This principle of law is set forth in at least seven multilateral human rights treaties: the United Nations (U.N.) Convention on the Rights of the Child [being one of these] . . ."

Promotes Premarital Sex for Teenagers

The broader agenda is to seek changes in the laws of each nation that will weaken the freedom and authority of parents to direct the moral education and attitudes of their children. Nowhere is there a suggestion in the CRC recommendations to signatory nations that the role of parents should be strengthened. . . .

Contraception for teenagers is a highly controversial issue, especially when governments advocate access for minors over the wishes of parents. Nowhere in U.N. committee comments or on its website does the organization propose abstinence until marriage. Instead, U.N. committees repeatedly urge that teenagers have:

1. Universal access to contraceptives and abortions without their parents' permission, and

2. Access to medical counseling services without their parents' consent.

For example, the U.N. committee urged Ireland to "improve family planning services and the availability of contraception, including for teenagers and young adults." Yet, since making contraception available to single people three decades ago, Ireland has [experienced soaring] rates of divorce, out-of-wedlock birth, sexually transmitted disease, violence, and abortion. . . .

The U.N. committees give similar advice to other countries, including Peru, Russia, the Maldives, Yemen, and Macedonia. . . .

U.N. interpretative committees argue that restricting abortion, even for teenagers, is a form of subordination that violates human rights. But there is little reason to believe that U.N. representatives and bureaucrats know better than individual societies how they should shape their own cultures and laws on family, marriage, sexual behavior, and the raising and education of children.

Children Should Not Be Forced into Labor

David L. Parker

An occupational physician, photographer, and author, David L. Parker has written and photographed several books and has received the Christopher Award for work affirming the highest values of the human spirit.

Many nations have written laws and treaties—such as the Universal Declaration of Human Rights and the Convention on the Rights of the Child—to protect children from economic exploitation. Children continue to be forced into labor, however; statistics estimate that more than 320 million children under the age of sixteen are currently working worldwide. Because labor is so detrimental to a child's health, education, and safety, all nations must commit to regulating child labor and protecting their children.

Seeking to protect children from what are often deplorable working conditions, national and international communities have implemented laws and treaties to regulate child labor. Since the United Nations [UN] General Assembly adopted the Universal Declaration of Human Rights in 1948, dozens of international treaties concerning children's rights have been written.

The most encompassing of these is the UN's 1989 Convention on the Rights of the Child, which recognizes every

David L. Parker, *Before Their Time: The World of Child Labor*, New York: Quantuck Lane Press, 2007. Copyright © 2007 by David L. Parker. Reproduced by permission.

child's right to a primary school education. The convention also requires that nations protect children from economic exploitation "and from performing any work that is likely to be . . . harmful to the child's health or physical, mental, spiritual, moral or social development."

Any job, even one that does not seem harmful, can keep a child from attending school.

Another important treaty, the International Labour Office's Prohibition and Immediate Action for the Elimination of the Worst Forms of Child Labor, known as Convention 182, took effect in 1999. The International Labour Office (ILO), a branch of the United Nations, brings governments, workers, and employers together to promote safer and healthier working conditions. Convention 182 defines the worst forms of work as those associated with slavery and bondage, prostitution and pornography, illicit activities such as the drug trade, and other work that "is likely to harm the health, safety, or morals of children."

Labor Undermines a Child's Education

In spite of numerous laws and treaties, child labor remains an enormous problem, and millions of children lack access to basic education. Officially, more than 320 million children under age sixteen work worldwide and 25 percent of children do not complete a primary school education. In addition, almost 150 million children labor in the worst forms of work as defined by the ILO.

I have sometimes found it difficult to define when work is harmful, in part because of the importance of education in all children's lives. Any job, even one that does not seem harmful, can keep a child from attending school. Education provides a basis for a child's social, economic, and cultural development as well as the foundation for a healthy life. Children whose parents—particularly their mothers—are better educated are more likely to go to school and stay in school longer than children whose parents received little or no education. Further, children with less-educated mothers are more likely to work at an earlier age than children with educated mothers.

For many families, child labor is part of an intergenerational cycle of poverty, social exclusion, and lack of education. Poor families frequently lack the resources to ensure that their children go to school and stay healthy. An increased risk of illness contributes to the cycle of poverty. Young women who work and go to school or who work instead of attending school tend to have less-healthy children. A woman who has been to school for even a few years is more likely to marry later, obtain prenatal care, have a smaller family, and have healthier, better-educated children.

Even jobs that seem relatively safe place children at risk.

Child Labor Is Often Abusive

Another difficulty in understanding when work is harmful stems from the complexity or ambiguity of some job circumstances. For example, in 1993 and 1995 I photographed circus performers in Nepal and India. Although the children are often laughing and having fun, most are bonded laborers, a type of modern-day slave. Circus owners trick families into selling their children and then force them to work many years without pay. Neither the poor working conditions nor the slavery-like situation is obvious to a casual observer.

Other forms of work harm children in much more obvious and painful ways. In 2000, I photographed children at a rehabilitation center for young combatants in Sierra Leone. The children told stories of being drugged and forced to kill their parents or mutilate their neighbors. They also reported being shot during combat or beaten if they tried to escape from military service.

Some domestic workers are held in virtual slavery behind locked doors. Although I have photographs of children doing domestic chores—preparing food, caring for sisters and brothers, and washing clothes—only once did I gain access to a private home where children were employed. The employer did not allow me to take photographs.

Overall, working conditions for most children are pathetic. Many work sites lack sanitary facilities and clean drinking water. Child workers are exposed to excessive noise, clouds of dust, and other safety hazards. They eat food they find on the street or in the garbage dump, drink water and bathe in the same pond where they wash their tools and mix mud for making bricks, and live on the street or in cardboard huts.

Because children are still developing physically and mentally, harmful substances have a greater impact on them than on older workers. Pound for pound, children breathe more air, eat more food, and drink more water than adults do. Toxic chemicals such as mercury or lead can cause brain damage and permanent disabilities.

Children work long hours with little time for rest, play, or school, and even jobs that seem relatively safe place children at risk. Street vendors may leave for work at four or five A.M. and not return home until late at night. They go long stretches without eating. They may be robbed or abused. Street children often work for unscrupulous adults who refuse to pay them, cheat them of their earnings, or sexually exploit them.

Children who work face a wide array of dangers, from rats, wild dogs, and rotting wastes in garbage dumps and choking dust in stone quarries to injuries from high-speed machinery or the harsh chemicals used to tan leather. Some [child laborers] develop diseases typically associated with adults, such as arthritis or skin diseases. Most children do not wear protective equipment. Even when such equipment is provided, it does not serve children well since it is designed for adults.

I am encouraged by new data indicating that the number of working children around the world has declined over the past few years. Some nations have made strides to protect child workers from dangerous conditions, yet many others still fail to keep children safe, healthy, and educated. . . .

Agricultural work is fraught with hazards, including chemical pesticides.

Labor in Agriculture Is Particularly Harmful

More children work in agriculture than in any other industry. In some nations up to one third of agricultural workers are children. The popular image of a child on a farm is that of someone playing happily in a haystack. Most people wrongly assume that farmwork is healthy and that children who work on farms are part of a family business.

In reality, agricultural work is fraught with hazards, including chemical pesticides, large machinery, venomous insects and reptiles, unsafe drinking water, and parasitic diseases from contaminated irrigation water. Children on farms, plantations, and fisheries work long hours doing heavy, exhausting work. They plow fields with tractors or oxen, pick vegetables, cotton, fruits, and grains, and dive for shellfish. Children work in fields that have just been sprayed with pesticides. They work all day under the beating sun. Some labor as slaves on cocoa plantations.

During a recent trip to Nicaragua, I visited tobacco plantations. Children working in these fields are exposed to high levels of nicotine, which is absorbed through the skin and causes nausea and vomiting. The children also experience pesticide poisoning, with similar effects. Living conditions on plantations are poor: A dozen or more men, women, and children typically share a small room with no running water.

In many countries, large migrant communities follow the agricultural seasons from one region to another. In the United States, migrants may start the year in Texas and gradually work their way to the sugar beet fields in Minnesota's Red River Valley or the vegetable canning plants in southern Minnesota. In Turkey, entire communities move from the eastern part of the country to central Anatolia to pick cotton, dig potatoes, or harvest vegetables. Common to all migrant communities are low wages, unhealthy sanitary facilities, and meager opportunities for education.

Children in coastal areas fish or help farm coastal waters. In Indonesia, up to two thousand fishing platforms, called *jermals*, rise from stilts in the ocean around Java and Sumatra. Labor contractors lure young workers from inland villages with promises of good wages. Because the platforms lie far out at sea the children cannot escape. Platform workers subsist on rice; fresh fruit and vegetables are a rare luxury and potable water is brought in just once a week. The bosses often subject the children to physical and sexual abuse.

In eastern Morocco, children wander the desert tending sheep and herding camels. Similarly, in India and Nepal, children feed and herd camels and other animals. Many of these children work alone all day. Although this may be a traditional way of life for some, these children miss out on the opportunities afforded by even a basic education. . . .

For every child who is freed from forced labor and inhumane work, there are many more who continue to work. International and national laws have gone a long way in creating an awareness of child labor. However, it will take commitment on the part of all nations to eliminate the worst of its forms. This commitment must provide for the basic needs of children, families, and their communities. These needs include schools, food, books, and health care.

4

Sweatshops Benefit Children and Their Families

Nicholas D. Kristof

Nicholas D. Kristof is a regular columnist for the New York Times, *a two-time Pulitzer Prize winner for journalism, and co-author of the book* Half the Sky: Turning Oppression into Opportunity for Women Worldwide.

Americans have good intentions when they advocate for strict labor standards and boycotts of products made in sweatshops. But despite the long hours and meager pay, sweatshops actually raise living standards for many workers in poor countries and provide a means out of poverty. Without sweatshops, more people— many of them children—would be scavenging on the streets for longer hours, under worse conditions, and for even less pay. In the long run, the best way to help is to promote sweatshops and encourage importing their products.

Before Barack Obama and his team act on their talk about "labor standards," I'd like to offer them a tour of the vast garbage dump here in Phnom Penh.

This is a Dante-like vision of hell. It's a mountain of festering refuse, a half-hour hike across, emitting clouds of smoke from subterranean fires.

The miasma of toxic stink leaves you gasping, breezes batter you with filth, and even the rats look forlorn. Then the smoke parts and you come across a child ambling barefoot,

Nicholas D. Kristof, "Where Sweatshops Are a Dream," *The New York Times*, January 15, 2009. Copyright © 2009, The New York Times. Reproduced by permission of NYT.

searching for old plastic cups that recyclers will buy for five cents a pound. Many families actually live in shacks on this smoking garbage.

Sweatshops Are Better than the Alternative

Obama and the Democrats who favor labor standards in trade agreements mean well, for they intend to fight back at oppressive sweatshops abroad. But while it shocks Americans to hear it, the central challenge in the poorest countries is not that sweatshops exploit too many people, but that they don't exploit enough.

Talk to these families in the dump, and a job in a sweatshop is a cherished dream, an escalator out of poverty, the kind of gauzy if probably unrealistic ambition that parents everywhere often have for their children.

"I'd love to get a job in a factory," said Pim Srey Rath, a 19-year-old woman scavenging for plastic. "At least that work is in the shade. Here is where it's hot."

Another woman, Vath Sam Oeun, hopes her 10-year-old boy, scavenging beside her, grows up to get a factory job, partly because she has seen other children run over by garbage trucks. Her boy has never been to a doctor or a dentist, and last bathed when he was 2, so a sweatshop job by comparison would be far more pleasant and less dangerous.

I'm glad that many Americans are repulsed by the idea of importing products made by barely paid, barely legal workers in dangerous factories. Yet sweatshops are only a symptom of poverty, not a cause, and banning them closes off one route out of poverty. At a time of tremendous economic distress and protectionist pressures, there's a special danger that tighter labor standards will be used as an excuse to curb trade.

When I defend sweatshops, people always ask me: But would you want to work in a sweatshop? No, of course not.

But I would want even less to pull a rickshaw. In the hierarchy of jobs in poor countries, sweltering at a sewing machine isn't the bottom.

Sweatshops can help people.

Sweatshops Raise Living Standards

My views on sweatshops are shaped by years [of] living in East Asia, watching as living standards soared—including those in my wife's ancestral village in southern China—because of sweatshop jobs.

Manufacturing is one sector that can provide millions of jobs. Yet sweatshops usually go not to the poorest nations but to better-off countries with more reliable electricity and ports.

I often hear the argument: Labor standards can improve wages and working conditions, without greatly affecting the eventual retail cost of goods. That's true. But labor standards and "living wages" have a larger impact on production costs that companies are always trying to pare. The result is to push companies to operate more capital-intensive factories in better-off nations like Malaysia, rather than labor-intensive factories in poorer countries like Ghana or Cambodia.

Cambodia has, in fact, pursued an interesting experiment by working with factories to establish decent labor standards and wages. It's a worthwhile idea, but one result of paying above-market wages is that those in charge of hiring often demand bribes—sometimes a month's salary—in exchange for a job.

In addition, these standards add to production costs, so some factories have closed because of the global economic crisis and the difficulty of competing internationally.

A Factory Is a Good Thing

The best way to help people in the poorest countries isn't to campaign against sweatshops but to promote manufacturing there. One of the best things America could do for Africa would be to strengthen our program to encourage African imports, called AGOA [African Growth and Opportunity Act], and nudge Europe to match it.

Among people who work in development, many strongly believe (but few dare say very loudly) that one of the best hopes for the poorest countries would be to build their manufacturing industries. But global campaigns against sweatshops make that less likely.

Look, I know that Americans have a hard time accepting that sweatshops can help people. But take it from 13-year-old Neuo Chanthou, who earns a bit less than $1 a day scavenging in the dump. She's wearing a "Playboy" shirt and hat that she found amid the filth, and she worries about her sister, who lost part of her hand when a garbage truck ran over her.

"It's dirty, hot and smelly here," she said wistfully. "A factory is better."

5

Girls Have Fewer Rights and Opportunities than Boys

Una Murray and Patrick Quinn

The people who work for the International Labour Organization (ILO), a specialized agency of the United Nations, make up the International Labour Office. Its aims are to advance opportunities for women and men so they can obtain decent and productive work in conditions of freedom, equity, security, and human dignity. Una Murray is a consultant for the IPEC (International Programme on the Elimination of Child Labour) and Patrick Quinn is from the Geneva, Switzerland, office of the IPEC.

In most countries throughout the world, boys are afforded more rights and opportunities than girls, often because cultures and societies have passed down from generation to generation the belief that males are more important and valuable than females. As a result, especially in poor countries where child labor is an economic necessity for many families, girls are more likely to be denied an education and forced into labor, thus limiting any chance of their own to rise out of poverty. When governments and policy makers assess and implement strategies in response to the global economic crisis, special attention should be given to the discrimination against girls and the risks they face as a result of that discrimination.

In many countries and cultures the opportunities enjoyed by boys and girls differ, from the earliest stages of life through childhood and into adulthood. In fact, there are very few countries, societies or communities where girls have exactly the same opportunities as boys.

Access to education is a human right, and an important foundation for an individual's future prosperity and welfare. Yet in much of the world boys and girls continue to be treated differently in terms of access to education. Parents often place more value on their sons' education than on their daughters', and girls therefore are often taken out of school at an earlier age than boys. The result of these inequalities in education can be seen in global literacy statistics. Of the 16 per cent of the world's population who are unable to read or write a simple statement, almost two out of three are women.

The role of females is often viewed as being of less importance or value than that of males.

The discrimination against girls in education often stems from the view that in later life boys will have better labour market opportunities, while girls will assume domestic responsibilities, marry and move to another family. The inequalities in access to education mean that by the time girls reach the minimum age of employment many are already at a social and economic disadvantage.

Male Work Roles Are Considered More Important

Children are taught from an early age to model themselves on their parents. In most societies different gender roles mean that boys and girls engage in different activities. For example, a person is not born with the ability to do needlework or cook but acquires such skills over time. In most cultures it is more likely that girls will be taught such "female skills" than boys.

The different patterns of work of males and females may vary from society to society, However, most boys and girls are eventually channelled into what are perceived as male or female work roles. Generally speaking, the role of females is often viewed as being of less importance or value than that of males. Girls are more likely to engage in types of work for which earnings are relatively low.

The opportunities that girls encounter early in life may well determine their chances later on. If girls lack basic education and engage in child labour at an early age they may be condemned to a future of poverty.

Much of the work undertaken by girls is less visible than that of boys. Sometimes [individuals] outside the family and close community may be altogether unaware of it. Typical examples are work on farms and in small-scale agriculture, domestic work and work in small home-based workshops.

The often hidden nature of domestic work has given rise to particular concerns. Girls engaged in domestic work are frequently reported as being treated poorly and sometimes being physically abused. Although some of these cases do become public, the fact that the work takes place within the confines of a private home means that abuse very often goes unseen and unreported.

This problem extends beyond domestic work. Girls working in many other situations also have little contact with others outside the immediate work environment, thus giving rise to concerns for their safety and welfare. Some of the worst forms of child labour may entail girls being deliberately hidden from the outside world. Girls trafficked for labour and prostitution, for instance, can sometimes be held as virtual prisoners.

All children involved in child labour are vulnerable. To begin with . . . chances are that they come from poor families. They often belong to a socially excluded community, such as an ethnic or indigenous group or a group with a subordinate station in the social hierarchy. They may live in rural areas where there are few facilities. All these factors create disadvantages which have an impact on boys and girls alike, but girls face additional challenges.

Many Girls Are Denied a Basic Education

In many societies, cultural norms and values place women in an inferior position, and this can result in girls being discriminated against in many ways. For example, girls and young women are more likely to lack basic education, which makes it more difficult for them to protect their rights. As girls enter the labour market, they may be directly discriminated against [by] being paid less than boys or being restricted to menial tasks.

Along with factors such as their relative lack of physical strength, the absence of protective legislation and a failure to enforce such laws that [do] exist, the particular vulnerability of girls may also derive from the work situation itself. A United Nations report on violence against children drew attention to the problem of violence against children at the workplace, including both verbal and physical abuse. The report identified a number of sectors in which violence can be a particular problem. Most of these were sectors in which girls work in large numbers. The report also indicated that incidents of violence against under-age workers are unlikely to be reported.

The term "double burden" is used to describe the workload of those who are not only engaged in an economic activity but also have responsibility for unpaid domestic work in their own household. Women and girls often spend significantly more time on household chores and caring duties, such as child-rearing or attending to the sick, than do their male counterparts. The obligation to undertake household chores inevitably limits the time available for education and other activities.

It is commonly assumed that in many countries, as young people start working, the boys go into paid or unpaid economic activity while the girls engage in domestic work in the home. In practice, however, as shall be seen later in this report, the picture is more complex. It appears in fact that during childhood years, girls are employed in economic activities almost as much as boys, but in addition they are expected to devote significantly more time than boys to domestic duties. . . .

A vicious circle connects poverty, lack of education and child labour. The children of the poor who become child workers are themselves likely to be poor as adults, and their children in turn will face limited access to education and may also end up in child labour.

Research shows that educating girls is one of the most effective ways of tackling poverty. Educated girls are more likely to earn more as adults, marry later in life, have fewer and healthier children, and have decision-making power within the household. Educated mothers are also more likely to ensure that their own children are educated, thereby helping to avoid future child labour. Tackling child labour among girls and ensuring their right to education are therefore important elements of broader strategies to promote development.

In addition to the economic benefits of an educated female labour force, there are major social gains to be had from investing in the education of girls. These social benefits accrue to the individuals themselves, to their families and to society at large, and are sustained over time. . . .

Girls entering the labour force may be unclear about their rights.

Girls Are Treated Unequally in the Labor Market

For young persons, especially those suffering from poor education or poverty, the transition to the labour market can be particularly difficult. If they are unable to continue in education, by the time they reach the minimum age of employment, girls may already be at a disadvantage compared to boys.

Adolescent girls receive a variety of conflicting and confusing messages on their gender role from their parents, teachers, peers and the media, and these can often be decisive in channelling girls into working at home or taking up some form of employment outside the home. Such decisions may well affect their future capacity to support themselves and other household members.

Girls entering the labour force may be unclear about their rights and responsibilities on issues such as recruitment processes, wage systems, hours of work and other working conditions.

Vocational training and skills development for young men and women can play an important role in the transition to work, but opportunities for training are often limited. In many cultures the training that is available to young women is still restricted to traditional "female" skills. Many of the courses that are organized for young women actually reinforce their traditional roles and responsibilities (for example, health, beauty and child-care courses). Such an emphasis reduces the chances of their entering careers or fields that are perceived as "unfeminine." Young women who may have the opportunity to move beyond traditional skills and into newer or non-traditional occupations can become more "employable" and possibly earn a better living too.

Social factors often put pressure on women to engage in training that gives them access only to low-productivity and low-paid jobs. Sometimes young women require much encouragement and strong incentives to sign up for courses which they may have been told are not appropriate for them. Moreover, because many young women may already be mothers or have caring responsibilities outside work, logistical arrangements must be carefully planned.

Informal or "traditional" apprenticeships are a major source of skills and training for work. However, traditional apprenticeships tend to benefit boys more than girls. Girls may be told that certain occupations are [appropriate only] for boys, and employers of apprentices may restrict their choice of apprentices to boys. Encouraging girls to undertake apprenticeships can assist them in moving into "nontraditional" areas of work in which earnings may be better.

Information about training and employment opportunities sometimes does not reach young women. This may be because information is conveyed through channels that are inaccessible to them, or because placement services are geared to a male clientele. Much recruitment is through informal contacts and networks, and if young women are excluded from them they will not receive information.

> *Investment in the education and training of girls can play a very important role in helping to break the poverty cycle.*

Many young women in the developing world have little choice but to get married early. Most young brides become young mothers. Apart from the health implications of early pregnancy, this restricts the access of young women to productive jobs. For young mothers, childcare and household chores tend to severely limit the possibility of further training or education. . . .

The Capability of Girls Is Undervalued

Girls and boys in situations of poverty are much more likely to be engaged in child labour than [youngsters] from more affluent families. Development policies that seek to reduce poverty and vulnerability of children are the key to achieving major and sustainable progress in tackling child labour. National poverty reduction strategies play an important role in determining the path of economic and social development in many developing countries, and it is important that issues of tackling child labour and promoting decent work for adults are integrated into such strategies.

Investment in the education and training of girls can play a very important role in helping to break the poverty cycle and should be a priority reflected in development plans and programmes. It is also important that plans and programmes address issues of gender inequalities in labour markets, which can limit the opportunities available to girls who have reached the minimum age of employment.

Social protection measures that target poor families can play an important role. Cash transfer programmes provide examples of resources being used to target and support vulnerable families, improving children's prospects of education and health care. Incentives such as school food programmes, which ensure that poor children receive a meal each day at school, can make the difference between a child being in school or in child labour.

The need to tackle child labour cuts across the mandate of many ministries. Ministries including those responsible for labour, education, finance, social affairs, women, children and youth should all have an interest in tackling child labour. Each should identify how [its] policies and programmes can be developed in order to support efforts to eliminate child labour and should give specific consideration to the situation of girls.

The provision of free, compulsory and quality education, at least up to the minimum age of employment, is the most important policy step a government can take to tackle child labour. Reducing the indirect cost of education (uniforms, books, transport, food, etc.) is also an important means of removing burdens that may otherwise prevent poor families from sending their children to school.

There are often specific barriers to girls' participation in education arising from cultural attitudes, safety concerns and the multiple disadvantages that girls may experience. Such barriers need to be identified at the national and local level so that appropriate strategies to tackle them can be identified and implemented.

Quality education requires a professional teaching force and a decent school environment. It is therefore important that national governments and donors support the education sector with adequate investment. There is a major worldwide shortage of teachers which needs to be tackled. Female teachers can serve as role models for girls and encourage their participation in education.

In developing education sector plans consideration must be given to those children who remain unreached by, or poorly served by, the education system. Children in child labour are a major part of this group. Available data and knowledge on child labour, including child labour among girls, can be used to support the targeting of children currently excluded from education. Good practices in tackling child labour among girls and promoting their education should be identified and scaled up into national initiatives. . . .

To support further policy and programme development, the knowledge base relating to the work of girls needs to be strengthened. This should include an in-depth analysis of the various aspects of child labour among girls, as well as of the relationship between child labour and the challenges facing adolescent girls in the labour market.

The global financial and economic crisis is pushing an increasing number of families into poverty. This could have a negative impact on child labour if families pull children out of school. When a poor family has to choose between sending either a boy or girl to school, in cultures in which a higher value is placed on boys education, girls are at particular risk of being pulled out of school.

Governments should ensure that measures implemented in response to the crisis do not have the effect of making the child labour situation worse. It is important that policy makers undertake an assessment of the possible employment, education and welfare implications of proposed recovery packages. The response to the crisis must include giving priority to budget expenditure that benefits poor and vulnerable households. Care must be taken to guard against the risk of both girls and boys being pulled out of school, and it should be noted that girls could be at special risk.

6

Female Genital Mutilation Violates Girls' Rights

Amnesty International USA

Founded in 1961 and the recipient of the Nobel Peace Prize, Amnesty International seeks to protect people wherever justice, freedom, truth, and dignity are denied. Through the organization's education, research, and action, governments have been persuaded to stop human rights violations.

Female Genital Mutilation/Cutting (FGM/C) is the removal of all or part of the female genitalia and subjects girls to excruciating pain, shock, infection, possible infertility, and sometimes even death. Predominantly practiced in twenty-eight North African countries, FGM/C is a traditional ritual that signifies the acceptance of a woman into society and her eligibility for marriage; it is rooted in a culture that aims to control women's sexuality and autonomy. Because the procedure clearly violates several basic human rights of girls, including the right to protection, health, gender equality, and physical integrity, many international treaties and conventions call for a worldwide strategy to end female genital mutilation.

I was genitally mutilated at the age of ten. When the operation began, I put up a big fight. The pain was terrible and unbearable . . . I was badly cut and lost blood . . . I was genitally mutilated with a blunt penknife. After the operation, no one was allowed to aid me to walk. . . . Sometimes I had to force myself not to urinate for fear of the terrible

Amnesty International USA, "Female Genital Mutilation/Cutting," February 2009. Reproduced by permission.

pain. I was not given any anesthetic in the operation to reduce my pain, nor any antibiotics to fight against infection.
Afterwards, I hemorrhaged and became anemic. This was
attributed to witchcraft. I suffered for a long time from
acute vaginal infections.

—Hannah Koroma, Sierra Leone

What Is Female Genital Mutilation/Cutting?

Female genital mutilation (FGM/C) is the removal of part, or
all, of the female genitalia. FGM/C may refer to clitoridectomy
(removal of the clitoris), excision (removal of the labia
minora), or infibulation (removal of the clitoris, labia minora
and majora, and stitching together).

FGM/C is a dangerous procedure that often results in dire
physical, sexual, and mental consequences. The procedure is
usually performed in unsanitary conditions, using objects like
broken glass, tin can lids, blunt knives, scissors, or razors. Victims are not given anesthesia or antibiotics and rarely have access to medical treatment. Infibulated women have their entire
external genitalia cut, scraped, or burned out. The subsequent
raw wound is stitched together with cat or lamb intestines or
thorns, leaving a small opening for the passage of menstrual
flow. The girl's legs are bound together for up to two months,
immobilizing her while the wound heals over.

Conducting such a major procedure in poor hygenic conditions often results in infection, shock, hemorrhaging, ab-
scesses, benign nerve tumors, cysts, excess scar tissue, progres-
sively enlarging scars, and sterility. Because FGM/C is practiced
as a group rite on many girls at once using the same cutting
implement, it can easily cause the spread of HIV and other
communicable diseases. Infibulation often causes a woman to
retain urine and menstrual blood, leading to chronic urinary
tract and pelvic infections that may cause sterility. Women
must be continually cut open for childbirth and resewn afterward, a process which results in a mass of thick scar tissue.

This makes childbirth not only excruciatingly painful, but also extremely dangerous as it prolongs labor, obstructs the birth canal, and often causes perianal tears in the mother. Such ill effects of FGM/C are rarely blamed on the practitioner, but are instead blamed on witchcraft or the inadequate performance of rituals associated with the procedure.

FGM/C is rooted in a culture of discrimination against women.

More than 130 million girls have been subjected to female genital mutilation/cutting. The practice, most prevalent in Africa and some countries in the Middle East, is also prevalent among immigrant communities in Europe, North America and Australia.

Why Is FGM/C Practiced?

FGM/C is traditionally practiced as a ritual signifying the acceptance of a woman into society and establishes her eligibility for marriage. It is believed to inspire submissiveness in young women. Reasons given for FGM/C range from beliefs that touching the clitoris will kill a baby during childbirth, to hygenic reasons, to enhancing fertility and ensuring chastity.

In many societies, an important reason given for FGM/C is the belief that it reduces a woman's desire for sex, therefore reducing the chance of sex outside marriage. In FGM/C-practicing societies it is extremely difficult, if not impossible, for a woman to marry if she has not undergone mutilation. Marriage is often the only role available for women in FGM/C-practicing societies because they receive little education and are discouraged from pursuing a profession. In the case of infibulation, a woman is "sewn up" and "opened" only for her husband. Family honor is seen as dependent on a woman's sexuality. Therefore, restricting women's sexuality is believed to be vital.

FGM/C is rooted in a culture of discrimination against women. It is a human rights abuse that functions as an instrument for socializing girls into prescribed gender roles within the family and community. It is therefore intimately linked to the unequal position of women in the political, social, and economic structures of societies where it is practiced.

Every day, thousands of girls are targeted for mutilation.

Alternatively, women who do not undergo FGM/C in societies where it is the norm are often ostracized by their communities and are considered ineligible for marriage. In countries where females are not adequately educated and are unlikely to find employment, unmarried women are often forced to rely upon relatives and the community and are denied the means to support themselves. Because marriage is seen as the only significant and acceptable role for women in FGM/C-practicing societies—and only women who are mutilated are eligible to marry—FGM/C reasserts women's relegation to the domestic sphere, conferring upon women an inferior status and reducing them to mere child-bearers and objects of . . . male sexual fulfillment.

Is FGM/C a Human Rights Violation?

Every day, thousands of girls are targeted for mutilation. FGM/C involves the deliberate infliction of severe pain and suffering, and its effects can be life threatening. FGM/C is often perpetrated on girls from birth to adolescence and is a grave violation of children's human rights. Most survivors must face physical and mental scars for the rest of their lives. Violence against women and girls in the home or in the community is regarded as a "private" issue; the fact that perpetrators are private actors rather than state officials has often precluded FGM/C from being seen as a human-rights concern.

FGM/C is a manifestation of gender-based human-rights violations that exist in all cultures that aim to control women's sexuality and autonomy. Though striking because of its severity and scale, FGM/C cannot be viewed in isolation. Recognizing that FGM/C is one of many forms of social injustice that women suffer worldwide is key to creating societies in which women are valued as full and equal participants.

A human-rights perspective sets FGM/C in the context of women's social and economic powerlessness. Recognizing that civil, political, social, economic, and cultural rights are indivisible and interdependent is a crucial starting point for addressing the range of factors that perpetuate FGM/C. A human-rights framework affirms that the rights of women to physical and mental integrity, to freedom from discrimination, and to the highest standard of health are universal. Violations of these rights can never be justified.

General Recommendation No.19 of the UN Convention on the Elimination of All Forms of Discrimination Against Women (CEDAW) asserts, "gender-based violence . . . is . . . violence that is directed against a woman because she is a woman or affects women disproportionately. . . ." States are obligated under international law to prevent, investigate, and punish violence against women. Out of the twenty-eight African countries that practice FGM/C, twenty-six have ratified *CEDAW*.

The UN Declaration on the Elimination of Violence Against Women recognizes that violence against women not only deprives them of their civil and political rights, but also their social and economic rights[; the document states] that, "the underlying structural consequences of these forms of gender-based violence help to maintain women in their subordinate roles, contribute to their low level of participation and to their lower level of education, skills, and work opportunities." The Declaration provides that states should not invoke any custom, tradition, or religious consideration to avoid their obligation to eliminate violence against women, and that they must exhibit due diligence in investigating and imposing penalties for violence, and establishing effective protective measures.

How Can FGM/C Be Stopped?

Local NGOs [nongovernmental organizations] recognize that in order for legislation to be effective, it must be accompanied by a broad and inclusive strategy for community-based education and awareness raising. In addition to creating, upholding, and enforcing anti-FGM/C legislation, states have the obligation to target the underlying beliefs and inequality that perpetuate the practice and reinforce gender-based discrimination. NGO's therefore augment states' legislation by working to eradicate FGM/C by providing education, medical treatment, and advocacy to women in FGM/C-practicing communities.

Some local organizations have designed alternative rite-of-passage rituals similar to the traditional FGM/C ceremonies that replace genital mutilation with gift giving and celebration. Key to an effective approach is the exercise of cultural sensitivity when dealing with a custom that has been prevalent for many years and is thought of as normal and necessary by cultures that practice FGM/C.

Effective action requires an understanding of the complexity of perceptions and beliefs surrounding FGM/C. The cultural significance of FGM/C cannot be ignored. Eradicating the practice needs to be understood as a question not of eliminating rites of passage, but of redefining or replacing those rites in a way that promotes positive traditional values while removing the danger of physical and psychological harm.

FGM/C is a practice that compounds unspeakable violence against women and young girls with discrimination, repression, and inequality. As the issue becomes more visible in the public sphere, states that allow FGM/C to be perpetuated face increasing criticism and scrutiny by the international community. It must be made clear that no form of violence against women can be justified by any cultural claim.

7

Children Have the Right to Comprehensive Sex Education

Barbara Miner

Barbara Miner is a columnist for Rethinking Schools *magazine and writes frequently on social issues.*

Children have the right to sex education, which in turn helps fulfill other basic rights, including their need to information about matters that affect them and the right to have their needs met. Effective comprehensive sex education should contain information detailing sexual development and reproduction, methods of birth control, sexually transmitted diseases and HIV, abortion, and the different religious and cultural views on sex and sexual diversity. Armed with such information, young people are better equipped to make choices regarding their behavior.

For the last decade, schools around the country have been badgered and bribed into pumping ideas into students' heads through abstinence-only programs—that is, those relatively few schools that teach sex education in the first place. Beginning under former-president Bill Clinton and escalating under President George W. Bush, more than $1.5 billion in federal and state money has been poured into abstinence-only education. These programs, by law, have as their "exclusive purpose" teaching about the benefits of abstaining from sexual activity; prohibit schools from talking about contraceptives and condoms; and define healthy sexuality as "a mutually faithful monogamous relationship in the context of marriage."

Barbara Miner, "We're Here. We're Sexual. Get Used to It," *Colorlines*, May–June 2008. Reproduced by permission.

Problems with Abstinence-only Education

Over the past year, this surging abstinence-only education movement has finally shown signs of retreat. Numerous studies have proven it to be ineffective, even harmful, and a growing list of states have turned down federal money when it comes with abstinence strings attached. But as abstinence fades, the increasingly pressing question is this: What will rise in its place? Sex education in public schools has never been a resource priority and has rarely been described as forward thinking. So will the half-hearted sex education that preceded abstinence return in coming years? Will there be anything at all? Or are this country's policymakers prepared to embrace a comprehensive sex education that goes beyond fear tactics and acknowledges that sexuality is a normal part of life, even for teenagers?

Schools' failure to help students understand and embrace their sexuality has particular consequence for kids of color, who represent vast majorities in many public schools around the country. Sex and race have always formed a volatile brew in America. Racist stereotypes of hypersexual men and women compete with restrictive mores, coming from both inside and outside of communities of color, to circumscribe sexual expression. Too many young people are left to sort through this maelstrom with little or no guidance, and too many don't find their way. Blacks and Latinos account for 83 percent of teen HIV infections. Similar disparities exist with nearly every other type of sexually transmitted infection—Black girls are more than four times as likely to get gonorrhea as their peers, and syphilis is skyrocketing among Black teenage boys and slowly climbing among Latino boys. Late last year, federal health monitors announced that teen pregnancy went up in 2006 for the first time in 15 years. The largest spikes were found among Black and Native American girls.

"In essence, our country has viewed youth as hormonally driven accidents waiting to happen, so we give them sex ed that censors information," frets James Wagoner, head of the Washington, D.C. group Advocates for Youth. "We adults tell them not to have sex until they're married, and never mind that none of us ever followed that advice."

Not only are the [abstinence-only] programs ineffective, but in many cases give kids inaccurate information.

The Beginnings of Abstinence-only Education

While most associate abstinence-only education with the [President George W.] Bush administration, such policies go back to 1981, when Congress started funding so-called "chastity education." The Supreme Court ultimately curtailed the programs because of their close association with religious proselytizing, but conservatives didn't stop organizing.

In 1996, abstinence-only found new footing when then-president Clinton signed welfare legislation onto which conservative activists had tacked abstinence-only education funding. Before long, abstinence-only efforts dominated school sex ed, even though no research had established the curricula as scientifically sound. [George W.] Bush expanded the programs and ratcheted up annual funding for them and then exported the idea by tying abstinence to foreign aid for HIV/AIDS initiatives.

Last year, that tide turned. The movement had always been controversial, but in April 2007 it was severely wounded when a comprehensive report found that students in abstinence-only programs were just as likely to have sex. An October report by the Government Accountability Office added that not only are the programs ineffective, but in many cases they give kids inaccurate information. That study reinforced a previous one by California Democrat Rep. Henry Waxman, that found several federally funded abstinence-only curricula were not only giving students inaccurate information, but were also pushing gender stereotypes—one program listed "financial support" as a "major need" for women and "domestic support" as one for men. And still more bad news came in December: While pregnancy and birth rates for U.S. teenagers had been falling since about 1991, there was an unexpected jump of almost 4 percent in 2006, according to a report by the National Center for Health Statistics.

The cavalcade of bad press emboldened states already uncomfortable with the programs. As of this February, 16 states had said they would no longer take federal funds for abstinence-only programs, which mandate states to partially match the federal dollars.

But that hasn't stopped the abstinence-only movement, which has grown into a nationwide industry of hundreds of politically connected groups receiving public dollars to push their scientifically suspect information on public schools. In an era of budget shortfalls, a disturbing number of schools say "yes" when the groups offer their abstinence-only curriculum for free. And while the abstinence movement may be wounded, Wagoner of Advocates for Youth warns that it is far from defeated. Powerful Democrats in Congress such as Dave Obey, the chairman of the House Appropriations Committee, have shown little concern about changing the abstinence-only approach.

"Politicians, including Democrats like Obey, are hypocritical when they demand responsible behavior from youth and then shut off all access to the information—access and support that they need," Wagoner argues. "That's not morality—it's irresponsibility and rank hypocrisy."

And what has been President [George W.] Bush's response to the raft of information disputing the merits of abstinence-only education? His proposed 2009 budget calls for $204 million in abstinence-only funding, including an increase of $28 million for the largest program, which is distributed through community-based groups.

Comprehensive Sex Education

Paul Zettel is a health education teacher at Riverside University High School in Milwaukee, Wisconsin, where more than 60 percent of the students are African American, 17 percent are Latino, and 8 percent are Asian. Special education students account for more than 15 percent of the students; there's a sizable group of English language learners, and most of the students are from low-income families. In other words, Riverside is a typical urban public high school.

Zettel teaches sex ed as part of a semester-long health class for sophomores, and his primary goal is to teach students the skills needed to make healthy decisions about their emotional, physical, intellectual and sexual health. A comprehensive sex ed approach that talks about contraception is only the first step, Zettel emphasizes. His students need far-broader support in developing healthy sex lives than just information on preventing STIs.

The entire paradigm, given the expectations within a sexist society, has to be challenged.

"People don't understand that our youth at Riverside are living in multiple health crises," Zettel says. "More than 30 percent are clinically depressed; one out of every two has been sexually assaulted by age 16. More than 15,000 students in the Milwaukee schools have a parent in prison or in jail on any given day, and kids come into class grieving because a friend was shot, or an uncle died. These epidemics are weighing our children down."

Milwaukee is no stranger to social problems. It consistently ranks in the top three of cities with the highest percent of births to teens and the highest child poverty rates. And then there's the staggering level of sexual assault in both the city and state. Juveniles accounted for the majority of sexual assault victims in 2001; almost half of girls younger than 15 said their first intercourse was nonconsensual; and about half of teenager mothers were sexually molested before their first pregnancy, according to a report last year from United Way of Greater Milwaukee.

Limitations of All Sex Education

One of the limitations of almost all sex ed, whether comprehensive or abstinence-only, is that it is based on fear: do this or else you'll get a disease, be careful or else you'll get pregnant and your life will be ruined. But there's another, often unmentioned, problem. Young women are rarely given the skills they need to resist unwanted sexual advances, especially from older boyfriends. Few sex ed classes teach students— either young men or young women—how to understand the difference between flirting and harrasment, or that the right to say "yes" to sex must also include the right to say "no."

"The entire paradigm, given the expectations within a sexist society, has to be challenged," says Ellen Bravo, the Milwaukee-based former director of 9to5, National Association of Working Women, who has been involved in anti-sexual-harassment training for more than 20 years. "We need to challenge the double standard that men with a lot of sexual experience are cool [but] women with a lot of experience are sluts and whores. Being sexual beings does not mean women have to be pressured into giving sexual favors, but that they have the right to a sexual relationship among equals."

But whether a Milwaukee sex ed class may invite Bravo in to discuss these issues is a matter of chance. While district policy nominally calls for comprehensive sex education, what does or doesn't happen in a particular school varies wildly—a confounding reality in school districts around the country.

"Overall, sex education in Milwaukee is definitely on the back burner," notes Jennifer Morales, a school board member who has two teenage sons in the public schools. She cites a number of factors for the haphazard nature of sex ed in

Milwaukee's schools: the out-of-control emphasis on testing; the year-after-year budget cuts; and the impossibility of teaching all the various curriculum mandates, whether from the reds, the state or the district: "I don't see any motion one way or another, either for more or less comprehensive sex ed. We've decentralized to the point where nobody is responsible for moving it forward, and we're in a morass."

And like many school districts, educators have little incentive and every reason to avoid becoming trailblazers. "There's a very real fear of public backlash if we push too hard on sex ed issues," Morales says. "We're not at the point where we have accepted that teenagers are sexual beings, and if you talk about that too much it's a one-way ticket out of teaching."

8

Children Should Be Taught Sexual Abstinence

Valerie Huber

Valerie Huber is the executive director of Parents for Truth and the National Abstinence Education Association.

Abstinence-centered sex education provides extensive information for adolescents regarding healthy and unhealthy relationships, skills development for decision-making, and sexually transmitted disease (STD) and risk avoidance strategies. Whereas comprehensive-based sex education encourages activities that put teens at risk for STDs and pregnancy, research has shown that abstinence education delays sexual onset and reduces sexual activity.

So common are sex scandals in Washington [D.C.], it comes as no surprise that the mainstream media hardly took notice when the Centers for Disease Control [and Prevention] (CDC) revealed disturbing news about teen sex in its Youth Risk Behavior Surveillance System (YRBSS) data for 2007.

Since 2005, mere teens are having sex, with more partners. Rates are up for teen pregnancies. Fewer young people are using condoms. This information runs parallel to the shocking statistic, released earlier this year [2008], that one in four teen girls has at least one STD [sexually transmitted disease].

For parents and public health officials, the YRBSS data signals a warning. In spite of increased HIV/AIDS education and millions of taxpayer dollars spent in the name of "comprehensive" sex education, teens remain at risk for the dangers associated with casual sex. The sex-saturated culture that sends the message that teen sex is expected and without consequence is often reinforced in sex education classes across the country, and so it comes as no surprise that risky behaviors are on the uptick.

Comprehensive Sex Education Undermines Abstinence

According to the Guttmacher Institute, 68 percent of public schools teach so-called comprehensive sex education. According to the U.S Department of Health and Human Services, comprehensive sex education programs spend less than 10 percent of class time promoting the merits of abstinence but an inordinate amount of time marginalizing the risks of casual sex.

In a section called "How to Make Condoms Fun and Pleasurable," the *Be Proud, Be Responsible* guidebook, a CDC-approved comprehensive sex education manual, invites students as young as 13 to "brainstorm ways to increase spontaneity" by encouraging teens to "eroticize condom use with a partner" and gives tips [such as] "use more lubrication," "act sexy and sensual" or "think up [a] sexual fantasy using condoms." The same guidebook also lists activities like showering together and body rubbing as "green light" activities.

Techniques taught in this contraception-based curriculum and countless others like it are encouraging activities that put teens at risk for STDs and other negative consequences. The new YRBSS data reveal the fall-out. Contraceptive sex education does not provide practical skills for maintaining or regaining abstinence but instead arms teens with sometimes explicit information that promotes gateway-to-intercourse activities.

When there is a shift in risky youth behavior, critics are quick to blame abstinence-centered education. After all, it did receive $174 million in federal funding last year. Abstinence education is an easy scapegoat for those who are ideologically opposed to it, but it can't be ignored that comprehensive sex education programs, which have received funding for the past 25 years, still receive more than double the funding that is given to abstinence education.

Abstinence Education Is Thorough

It is time that taxpayers and parents receive an accounting for the proliferation of harmful contraceptive sex education programs in our schools. That is why NAEA [National Abstinence Education Association] recently launched its Parents for Truth Campaign (www.parentsfortruth.org). Youth should no longer reap the devastation caused by the dangerous messages of this failed public health approach. Teens deserve the risk avoidance strategies [detailed] in abstinence education.

Within an abstinence education program, teens receive all the information they need in order to make healthy choices.

Abstinence-centered education, as funded by Congress, is decidedly more inclusive than "just say no." The term, "abstinence only" is strategically attached to this funding by opponents to create the false perception that abstinence education is a narrow and unrealistic approach. Abstinence education is overwhelmingly more comprehensive and holistic than other approaches and focuses on the real-life struggles that teens face as they navigate through the difficult adolescent years.

Abstinence education realizes that "having sex" can potentially affect a lot more than the sex organs of teens, [and,] as research shows, can also have emotional, psychological, social, economic and educational consequences. That's why topics frequently discussed in an abstinence education class include how to identify a healthy relationship; how to avoid or get out of a dangerous, unhealthy, or abusive relationship; developing skills to make good decisions; setting goals for the future and taking realistic steps to reach them; understanding and avoiding STDs; information about contraceptives and their effectiveness against pregnancy and STDs; practical ways to avoid inappropriate sexual advances and why abstinence until marriage is optimal.

So, within an abstinence education program, teens receive all the information they need in order to make healthy choices. And all of these topics are taught within the context of why abstinence is the best choice.

Research shows that abstinence education delays sexual onset, helps sexually experienced teens discontinue their sexual activity, and helps currently sexual active teens reduce [their] number of partners while using condoms at the same rate as their peers.

As lawmakers begin to debate funding levels for the public health of American's youth, Congress will consider the YRBSS data. Lawmakers must recognize the growing body of research that affirms abstinence-centered education is effective, and they must honor the 80 percent of American parents who, despite political ideology, support continued funding for abstinence education.

9

Minors Should Have the Right to Consent to an Abortion

Caitlin Borgmann

Caitlin Borgmann is a professor at the City University of New York School of Law and is the editor of the Reproductive Rights Prof Blog.

On July 14, 2009, Illinois joined thirty-four other American states in mandating parental notification before a teenager can obtain an abortion despite evidence that such a restriction is irrational, often unnecessary, and sometimes harmful. At a time when most states recognize the rights of minors to choose their own sexual and reproductive health care, mental health services, and alcohol and drug abuse treatment, it should appear obvious that the ultimate goal of parental notification laws is not to involve parents but to eliminate abortion altogether. Teenage girls—especially ones who lack loving and supportive parents—should have the right to an abortion without parental consent. Their lives could be in danger without it.

On July 14 [2009], in *Zbaraz v. Madigan*, the Seventh Circuit lifted a permanent injunction that had prevented enforcement of Illinois' parental notice for abortion law since its enactment in 1995. The decision hinged on an arcane question of state procedural law, and the opinion did not break new legal ground on the abortion issue. What is noteworthy

Caitlin Borgmann, "Abortion Parental Notice Laws: Irrational, Unnecessary and Downright Dangerous," *Jurist*, July 27, 2009. Reproduced by permission.

about the decision, then, is precisely what for many might seem mundane: Illinois will now join the ranks of 34 other states in enforcing some kind of parental involvement requirement before a teenager can obtain an abortion. The court emphasized the unexceptional nature of its decision, noting that "[m]any, if not all of the concerns first raised against parental involvement laws in the 1970s and early 1980s have been addressed" in laws like Illinois'.

Teens who avoid telling their parents often have compelling reasons for doing so.

The Irrationality of Parental Involvement Laws

This soothing language, however, obscures the fact that a substantial majority of states blithely impose what are in reality irrational laws that impose appalling burdens on the teenagers who are least able to consult with their parents about their pregnancies. States continue to enforce these restrictions despite evidence that they do not serve their intended purpose . . . and are unnecessary for most teens and downright dangerous for others. It is worth a pause to reflect on these laws that now seem scarcely to merit a yawn from the courts.

On their face parental involvement laws appear intended to keep parents informed and to ensure minors' wellbeing. But let's remember that the main proponents of parental involvement laws oppose abortion altogether. Their ultimate goal is not to improve familial communication but to eliminate abortion as an option for all women. A strategy memo written by anti-abortion-rights movement leaders James Bopp, Jr., and Richard E. Coleson, for example, encourages the passage of "parental involvement" laws, among other "incremental" restrictions on abortion. They argue that such laws "keep the abortion issue alive and . . . also translate into more disfavor for all abortions, which in turn reduces abortions."

Parents understandably want to be involved in their minor children's important life decisions, but this desire has not translated to parental involvement requirements for other sensitive medical decisions that minors make. Most states recognize that mandating parental involvement for sensitive medical treatment will have the hazardous drawback of deterring many minors from seeking care at all. As the Guttmacher Institute reports, "The legal ability of minors to consent to a range of sensitive health care services—including sexual and reproductive health care, mental health services and alcohol and drug abuse treatment—has expanded dramatically over the past 30 years." Minors in most states can consent to services such as contraception, prenatal care, and treatment for sexually transmitted infection. In many states, minors can even relinquish their children for adoption and consent to medical care for their children. Parental involvement laws for abortion stand out as the glaring antithesis to this trend.

Studies have shown that most pregnant teens voluntarily involve their parents in their abortion decisions. Even in the absence of a parental involvement law, about six in ten teens consult at least one parent before seeking an abortion. Teens who avoid telling their parents often have compelling reasons for doing so. Teenagers may suffer abuse when their parents discover they are pregnant; other teens are thrown out of the house. Some parents actively prevent their children from obtaining an abortion. Some minors function as the *de facto* adult in dysfunctional homes where the custodial parent is largely absent. Because of the dangers that minors can confront when forced against their own judgment to involve their parents, most major medical groups, including the AMA [American Medical Association] and the American Academy of Pediatrics, oppose mandating parental involvement for abortion.

The Futility of the Judicial Bypass

The [U.S.] Supreme Court has held that teenage girls, like adult women, have a constitutional right to determine the fate of their pregnancy. Thus, while states can require parental consent or notice for abortion, the Court requires that they provide some alternative for teens who do not wish to consult their parents. The alternative that has become standard is the judicial bypass. The judicial bypass allows a teenager to seek permission from a court rather than involve her parents in her decision. Not surprisingly, this option holds many perils for a pregnant teenager. Teens must navigate the process of a court hearing. They must find the time, often during school hours, to appear in court before an imposing stranger to discuss this most intimate of issues. Although the Supreme Court has required that the process be confidential, in practice it can be difficult for teens to keep their presence secret. In small towns, they may know the court personnel. In one instance, a teen waiting in the hallway for her hearing encountered her sister's entire class, which had come to the courthouse on a field trip.

Ironically, properly functioning bypass systems demonstrate the irrationality of requiring court waivers in the first place. When bypass processes work as envisioned, the vast majorities of minors' petitions are granted. This is because the law requires that judges must grant a waiver of parental involvement if a minor is either mature enough to consent on her own or if an abortion without notice would be in her best interests. The vast majority of minors fall into one of these two categories. For example, one study in Massachusetts showed that out of 477 petitions, only one minor was denied a waiver. Indeed, a report by the AMA found that minors' decision making process on abortion is comparable to that of adults aged 22–25. Thus, when bypasses work correctly, they ensure nothing more than that minors needlessly parade through courtrooms in order to be granted the right to do what they can already do for a host of other sensitive medical treatments: provide their own consent.

On the other hand, bypass processes often don't work. Helena Silverstein's book, *Girls on the Stand: How Courts Fail Pregnant Minors*, documents the myriad ways in which the bypass process can fail. Court personnel are often misinformed about the procedures. Some judges ignore confidentiality requirements. Other judges, ideologically opposed to abortion, refuse to hear bypass petitions, or they conduct hearings but then lecture teens about their immorality and routinely deny waivers. In these all too frequent circumstances, the "bypass" becomes a roadblock. While minors facing such roadblocks can try to seek an abortion in another state, not all will be able to do so. As the Guttmacher Institute points out, "[t]o travel out of state, a minor must have access to transportation and must be within a reasonable distance of a state with less restrictive laws. The degree to which minors exercise this option varies by age, socio-economic status and access to public transportation."

The *Zbaraz* court conceded that the bypass process may be "intimidating" and may pose "practical problems" for many minors. However, the court demurred, "[W]e fail to see a better alternative." This is a cop-out. The court may have felt compelled to follow precedent, but it should not pretend that precedent dictated a good outcome. Healthcare providers should always strongly encourage teens to involve their parents in their abortion decisions. But laws like the one that will now be enforced in Illinois do nothing to help teenagers, while imposing traumatic hurdles, and sometimes grave danger, on those who lack loving and supportive parents to whom they can turn.

10

Middle School Students Should Have Access to Birth Control

Abigail Jones and Marissa Miley

Abigail Jones, a reporter and staff writer, cowrote the book Restless Virgins: Love, Sex, and Survival at a New England Prep School *with Marissa Miley. Marissa Miley's work has appeared in* Esquire *and* USA Today, *and she was the content writer for Harvard University's Initiative for Global Health.*

It is a fact: Boys and girls as young as age eleven are engaging in sexual activity. Facing up to that fact, school officials in Portland, Maine, decided to provide birth control and sexual counseling to their middle-school students. Many people are concerned about that decision, partly because they do not want to admit that their kids are having sex, and partly because they believe parents should be notified if their children receive birth control. Nevertheless, the Portland school officials made the right choice because now their students will be better equipped when making decisions about their sexual activity.

Congratulations, Portland, Maine, for voting to provide birth control and counseling about sexually transmitted diseases (STDs) to middle schoolers. You are no longer a victim of the generational chasm between adults and teenagers. You've admitted what so many deny: teens are sexually active, and we need to help them stay safe and make smart choices.

Abigail Jones and Marissa Miley, "On Providing Birth Control for Middle Schoolers," The Huffington Post, October 19, 2007. Reproduced by permission of the authors.

The Truth About Kids and Sex

No matter how innocent we want middle schoolers to be, the truth is that girls and boys aged 11, 12, 13, and 14 years are hooking up, performing oral sex, and having intercourse. Not everyone is, but even when a student chooses not to engage in these behaviors, his or her friends or classmates may be. To anyone who disagrees, here's a reality check:

"One [youth in eight is] sexually experienced, having engaged in intercourse, oral sex or both before the age of 14," the *Journal of Adolescent Health* reported in 2006. According to the Project Connect study, supported by the Centers for Disease Control and Prevention:

- "9 percent reported ever having sexual intercourse . . . and 8 percent ever had oral sex (active or receptive)."

- "Of those who reported intercourse, 36 percent were age 11 or younger at first sex, 27 percent were 12, 28 percent were 13, and 9 percent were 14 or older."

- "Alarmingly, 43 percent of sexually experienced participants reported multiple sex partners."

Note that more girls and boys had sex at age 11 than age 12, at age 13 than age 14. If this data doesn't convince you, here are a few more findings. These examples may not be about intercourse, but they illuminate the over-sexed landscape in which girls and boys are growing up today.

One of the girls in *Restless Virgins: Love, Sex, and Survival at a New England Prep School*, a nonfiction book about seven high school students, had her first sexual experience in sixth grade—with sex dice. One die listed body parts (neck, lips), and another listed actions (lick, suck); all she had to do was roll and follow the instructions.

Last October, Tesco, the U.K. [United Kingdom] mega store, was forced to pull a pole-dancing kit from the toys and games section of its Web site, frequented by moms, dads, and, most importantly, young girls and boys. The toy came in a pink plastic tube, had featured bubble letters and a Barbie-type character, and said, "Unleash the sex kitten inside."

And just recently, we heard that the latest bar mitzvah gift is a blowjob at the back of the bus on the way to the DJ [disc jockey] party.

It's all startling to us, too, and we're the ones who just spent over two years immersed in teenage life, listening to guys brag about their sexual conquests and girls convince themselves that they really did want to give that guy—who didn't call or like her enough—oral sex. But there's a difference between being startled and being in denial.

Providing birth control to sexually active middle schoolers is a crucial step.

The Choice Between Informing Parents and Protecting Children

Some opposing the Portland decision argue that 11-year-olds should not be given birth control without a parent's consent. It's a fuzzy line. Of course parents should be involved in their children's health care. Of course they should know whether . . . their sons and daughters are having sex. It's easy to tell adults to talk with teens about sex, but it's another thing to actually do it.

The generational chasm we mentioned above is very real and very wide. We get it: a mother may not want to admit that her 12-year-old daughter is having sex in her boyfriend's basement after school. But that mother needs to know this is going on. So what about girls and boys whose parents don't know—or don't want to face—their children's sex lives?

Thank goodness for Portland, Maine.

Providing birth control to sexually active middle schoolers is a crucial step. Condoms and the pill don't protect against

STDs, but [these measures] will prevent girls from getting pregnant and lower the risk of transmitting many diseases. Providing counseling is just as critical. As we discovered, teenagers know about STDs and condoms. They've had sex ed. They're familiar with the Rolodex [a compact office filing system] of ramifications, and younger girls and boys need to be, too. And what all of them need is education about the emotional consequences of their sexual behavior.

How will you feel after giving a guy, who's not your boyfriend or even your friend, oral sex?

Do you really want to hook up with those two guys, at the same time, while another friend watches? You do? Okay, why?

These are tough questions, but they're not asked enough, if at all. Girls and boys are coming of age in a culture that's saturated by sex. They're affected by this culture, and they need the tools to make the right decisions. This isn't about religion or moral judgment. This is about protecting young people who are already engaged in sexual behavior. Thankfully, girls and boys in Portland, Maine, will now have access to birth control and counseling, and therefore be more equipped to make smarter and safer decisions about their sexuality. It's time for other school districts to wake up and take notice.

11

Middle School Students Should Not Have Access to Birth Control

Amy Topolewski

Amy Topolewski, a 2009 graduate of the University of Michigan at Dearborn, studied journalism and health policy and was a staff columnist for the school newspaper, the Michigan Journal.

Because seventeen pregnancies were reported at middle schools in Portland, Maine, the city's school officials voted to make a full range of birth control available to their students, with or without parental knowledge. The problem is not that middle school students are getting pregnant, however; the problem is that these students—eleven- and twelve-year-olds—are having sex in the first place. Instead of encouraging children to engage in sexual activity by providing them with birth control, parents and teachers should provide counseling to prevent sexual activity from happening at all.

"Birth control is just offering protection. It is no different than giving out bike helmets or immunizations."

These are the disturbing words of one reader in response to reading a *USA Today* article about offering birth control pills to girls as young as 11. I hardly think that you can equate riding a bike with having sex, but especially not at the age of 11.

On Oct. 18 [2007], school officials in Portland, Maine voted to make birth control pills available to students at one of the city's middle schools. King Middle School will be Maine's first school to have a full range of contraception available, including birth control pills, patches and condoms. Condoms have been offered by the school since 2000.

Providing contraception to children this young is not getting at the root of the problem.

Perhaps the condoms have been ineffective (or too big for the pre-pubescent bodies of 11- and 12-year-olds), because the decision to offer oral contraceptives to girls is based on 17 reported pregnancies at Portland's three middle schools in the last four years.

Not Confronting the Real Problem

If condoms have been available to students over the last four years and didn't prevent pregnancies, what makes school officials believe that birth control pills or patches will be any more effective in preventing pregnancy? If the availability of condoms didn't work, perhaps girls, who are said to mature faster than boys, will be responsible enough to remember to take the pill every day. No 11- or 12-year-old child, whether girl or boy, should be held responsible for weighing the consequences—emotional and physical—of having sex.

The truth of the matter is this: Providing contraception to children this young is not getting at the root of the problem. The problem is not that girls are becoming pregnant, though this is a horrifying reality. Rather, the problem is that 11-year-olds are having sex at all. This problem is being ignored. Instead of offering counseling to attend to the larger problems that are surely at work in the life of an 11-year-old who is having sex, school officials have found a way to treat only the symptoms.

Another problem with this decision is that treatment at the school's health center is confidential under state law. Though children would need to have their parents' permission to seek treatment at the clinic (which also treats the common cold or headaches), parents would not necessarily know if their child was prescribed birth control pills or given other forms of contraception. The only way parents would be aware is if their child came to them and told them.

The board's decision sends the message that having sex at this age is OK.

This decision is said to have been made largely because parents are not doing their jobs. Agreed. But this decision is just putting up another wall between parents and children by leaving parents out of the loop when it comes to the sexual activities of their children.

Encouraging Sexual Activity

The controversy over the decision [revolves] largely around the idea of whether . . . it encourages promiscuity among students. It is too soon to test the validity of this idea, but undoubtedly the availability of contraception magnifies the fact that there are indeed children as young as 11 or 12 having sex. It makes students who have not yet even given a thought to the opposite sex much more aware of the idea. At such a young and impressionable age, who's to say that this new awareness will not increase their curiosity concerning sex?

The availability of contraception may also provide students with a false sense of security. Though no form of birth control completely guards against pregnancy or STDs, children may get the idea that by using contraception, they are immune to any negative consequences of sex. The board's decision sends the message that having sex at this age is OK as long as protection is used. Ultimately, this decision is wrong.

During the 2006–2007 school year, five of 134 students who visited King's health center admitted having had sex, according to the lead nurse in the city's school health centers. So, instead of focusing on the 129 students who have not ventured down the road of sexual activity, the board has put all students at risk for the sake of five. It's not that these five students are insignificant. If anything, they, 11- and 12-year-olds having sex, need counseling, not birth control.

12

Random Drug Testing Violates Students' Rights

Debra J. Saunders

Debra J. Saunders is a conservative columnist whose work has appeared in the San Francisco Chronicle, Wall Street Journal, National Review, *in other mainstream publications, and on Web sites.*

Government should be kept out of family decision-making and parental responsibility, including the issue of student drug use. Because drug tests for all students would violate many edicts set forth in the U.S. Constitution (such as the presumption of innocence and the need for probable cause before conducting searches), court and school officials used a pretense of safety to begin testing student athletes for drugs. And then the officials— including the U.S. Supreme Court—stretched the justification for drug testing to cover any student who engages in extracurricular activities. Random student drug testing is wrong; it does not work, and it should be stopped.

In America, where citizens are supposed to want to keep government out of their family decision-making, there should be no random drug testing at public schools. Yet some 19 percent of public schools engage in some form of student drug testing, the University of Michigan's *Journal of School Health* found in 2003. President [George W.] Bush proposes to spend $25 million in 2006 to fund more random drug testing. And the internationally minded U.S. Supreme Court thinks that drug testing in public schools is just swell.

This is wrong. Parents who suspect their children of using drugs are free to test their kids. Hence, there is no need for schools to intervene—any more than there is a need for schools to set the punishment for children who disobey their parents' rules. Except that it is happening.

It would be a coercive violation of privacy rights to force all public-school students to submit to drug tests.

How It Started

It started when schools began testing athletes; there was at least the pretense of a safety argument for the tests—you don't want stoned kids leaping for a high fly [a tricky catch in baseball]. But by the time the U.S. Supreme Court ruled on said tests in 1995, the rationale for the tests had expanded. The [justices on the high court's] Big Bench supported testing of athletes to prevent the "increased risk of sports-related injury," but also because athletes are role models.

Court and school officials understand that it would be a coercive violation of privacy rights to force all public-school students to submit to drug tests. It goes against the presumption of innocence, unreasonable searches, the need for probable cause and other quaint notions found in the U. S. constitution. So those officials who want the government to play parent have come up with a new angle—require students who engage in extracurricular activities to agree to random drug testing. It's not mandatory, they argue, because students don't have to join clubs. And believe it or not, [in 2002 the U.S. Supreme court agreed].

The surest bet in America is: Once a bad idea is born, it only gets bigger.

Testifying before a House committee in February [2005], Bush drug czar John Walters argued that school "drug testing can be done effectively and compassionately." Its purpose, he explained, "is not to punish students who use drugs, but to prevent use in the first place, and to make sure users get the help they need to stop placing themselves and their friends at risk."

It Does Not Make Sense

[The problem] is: It is not clear how many students don't use drugs because they want to be in the chess club. Probably some students refrain. Still, University of Michigan researcher Lloyd Johnston noted in 2003 that there is "a serious question of whether drug testing is a wise investment," as it is not clear that it deters student drug use.

I don't think it is good policy to treat innocent students as if they might be guilty by making them pee in a cup if they want to be in debate club.

Meanwhile, there can be little doubt that students who use drugs say no to extracurricular activities because they don't want to say no to drugs. Testing for club membership, said Tom Angell of Students for Sensible Drug Policy, pushes these students "away from those positive atmospheres that study after study has shown are successful at keeping students away from drugs."

It's twisted: The very do-gooders who first lament that drug use consigns students to do poorly in school, now push for policies that marginalize students and guarantee that they will not have a full high-school experience.

And it doesn't matter what parents think. When the Supreme Court ruled in favor of testing for students who sign up for extracurricular activities in 2002, I asked the National School Board Association what it thought of a policy that required testing of students, even if parents took the responsibility. "The answer is that your child cannot participate in extracurricular activities," an official answered. "It's not negotiable."

Lori Earls, the parent of an Oklahoma high-school student on the losing side of the 2002 case, was outraged by the school's drug policy. She believed that other parents supported drug testing because it relieved them of the responsibility of their children's drug use, and ceded it to the schools. "They took away the parents' job," she noted.

And yet there is no outcry.

13

Students Should Be Tested for Drugs

David G. Evans

David G. Evans, executive director of the Drug Free Schools Coalition, is a member of the Student Drug-Testing Coalition. He also authored a successful amici curiae brief submitted to the Supreme Court in the case that expanded random student drug testing coverage to all students involved in extracurricular activities.

It is important that schools provide a safe environment for children so they can learn and grow academically, emotionally, and socially. The presence of drugs destroys that environment. And so, after an alarming number of students began using and selling drugs on school campuses, the U.S. Supreme Court ruled in favor of random drug testing for students involved in athletics and extracurricular activities. The goal is to deter drug use and protect the health and safety of students, a goal that far outweighs any cry of privacy violation.

Recently [2002], the United States Supreme Court came out with a commonsense ruling in favor of student drug testing. The Court decided that the health and safety of schools and students outweighed an individual student's minimal privacy interest when it comes to drug testing. The Court upheld a school drug testing program that permitted random testing of students in athletics and extracurricular activities such as clubs. The Court spoke of the drug use "epidemic" that is de-

David G. Evans, "Student Drug Testing Works," Student Drug-Testing Coalition, December 30, 2006. Reproduced by permission.

stroying the lives of thousands of children a year and wreaking havoc with their families. In the face of this destruction, the Court said that it is reasonable to use drug testing to deter drug use as we do in the military, workplace, criminal justice system, and professional athletics.

Drugs Are Insidious

When drugs invade a school, threatening the safety of students and disturbing the orderly learning environment, the school's interest in ridding the school of drugs outweighs the privacy interests of students. The school years are a critical passage in a young person's life. While in school, children face the challenge of learning in the academic, social, physical, and emotional realms. When drugs infect a school it cripples the learning process. Children become casualties. The physical and psychological effects of drug and alcohol use can cause lifelong and profound losses. Substance use decreases a child's chances of graduation and academic success.

Researchers continually report statistics demonstrating that student drug and alcohol use is at a dangerous level. For example, the National Center on Addiction and Substance Abuse (CASA) at Columbia University in New York City reports that for the last six years schoolchildren in the USA have listed drugs as the most important problem they face.

A 1997 CASA survey revealed that high school students see more drug deals at school than in their neighborhoods. In the survey, 76% of high school students claim that drugs are kept, used, or sold on school grounds. In addition, 29% of high school students claim that a student in their school died from a drug- or alcohol-related incident in the past year.

CASA also reports that substance abuse adds at least $41 billion dollars to the costs of elementary and secondary education in terms of special education, teacher turnover, truancy, property damage, injury, counseling, and other costs.

According to a study in the *Journal of the American Medical Association*, students who use drugs are more likely to bring guns and knives to school, leading to school violence. According to the New Jersey Department of Education report, assaults are up 30% with school staff as victims in 19% of the cases.

Students report that drug testing gives them a reason to say "no" to drugs.

Random Drug Testing Benefits All Students

Random drug testing is intended to give schools a stronger weapon to get drugs out of schools. School drug-testing programs are a proven low cost method to win the fight for our children's future. Consider the results of random drug testing of athletes at Hunterdon Central Regional High School in Flemington, New Jersey, USA. After two years of testing they experienced a decline in 20 of 28 categories of drug use in the whole student population. Studies in Oregon and Indiana in the USA also show substantial reductions in drug use due to testing.

The critics of testing claim that giving drug tests to students who participate in extracurricular activities will make the activities less attractive to students. They claim that by having less participation in extracurricular activities that students will choose to participate in drug-related behavior. While it is true that extracurricular activities help students to lead a positive life, there is no evidence that there is a drop-off in participation because of drug testing. In fact, students report that drug testing gives them a reason to say "no" to drugs. We must remember that the majority of kids do not use drugs!

The Court based its reasoning, in part, on the fact that these extracurricular activities are voluntary. If students wish to avoid a drug test, they can do so easily by not participating in these activities. We want students to make choices such as "do I use a drug or do I stay on the football team?" Our experience is that students choose the extracurricular activity over the drug. During the first year of random testing, the Hunterdon Central [High School] football team won the state championship. The coaches reported that the students were doing better in practice, and the students reported that drug testing gave them the opportunity to avoid drug parties.

Some critics say that extracurricular activities are a requirement to get into college and [that] students should not be forced to choose between extracurricular activities and their beliefs about their privacy. School-based extracurricular activities are not needed to get into college. There are many activities outside of school, such as athletics, plays, competitions like chess clubs, or service work.

Student testing should also include alcohol, although there is less need for alcohol testing because it is usually apparent when someone is under the influence of alcohol, which is not always the case with drug use.

Privacy Is Protected

The goals of random drug testing are to deter drug use and, if a student is detected as using drugs, to offer education and treatment to the student. The goal is not to punish students. This was specifically noted by the Supreme Court in approving such programs.

Student confidentiality is protected by two important federal laws. The first is the Family Educational Rights and Privacy Act. [It] prohibits student records from being released, including drug and alcohol testing results, without the consent of the parents or, if the student is 18, without the student's consent. Student treatment records are protected by the federal Alcohol and Drug Patient Regulations that carry federal criminal penalties for improperly releasing information.

Drug testing is not the final solution. Certainly we need to continue efforts at education and resolving our cultural problem with drugs. Drug testing only works when included in treatment and education.

For every student who claims that privacy is violated by having to take a drug test, we can show . . . parents who have buried their children because of drugs. [Schools] must be allowed to fulfill their mission of educating students and protecting [students'] health and safety. Drug testing is a valuable tool in achieving these goals.

14

Children Have the Right to Be Protected from Bullying

Ceil Than

Ceil Than is a writer, editor, and educator who has published fiction and nonfiction on a variety of topics.

A child who deliberately and consistently uses physical assault or verbal abuse to inflict fear or harm is a bully. Usually this behavior can begin as early as age eight, can be found in boys or girls, can take place anywhere children gather (including the Internet), and can cause extreme suffering and long-lasting emotional devastation for its victims. Because every child has the right to feel safe, parents, teachers, and school officials must learn to recognize the warning signs of bullying and create effective policies for dealing with and preventing such behavior.

Ask a twelve-year-old what he or she hates most about school, and you might be surprised to learn that the school bully outranks homework and tests on the fear-factor scale. A bully is a child who deliberately and [continually] uses physical assault or verbal abuse to harm another child that he or she sees as more vulnerable. Bullies and their victims can be as young as eight years old, and school bullying peaks in the high school years. Bullies and their victims can be boys or girls, and bullying can take place in cyberspace as well as [on] the schoolyard. Both the bully and his or her victim suffer, and some are driven to extreme or suicidal behavior.

Ceil Than, "'Wanna Fight?' Bullies and Their Victims Disarmed," Children's Rights of New York, Inc. *HOTLINE*, vol. 29, Spring 2008, pp. 1–3. Reproduced by permission.

According to a survey done by the American Academy of Child and Adolescent Psychiatry, 50% of school age children report being bullied at some point during their school years, and 10% report being bullied [continually]. Children in this age group are most intensely aware of their peers' opinions, acceptance, and rejection. The experience of being singled out and picked on can turn into an even more emotionally devastating downward spiral, and the experience of power felt by a bully can also become a dangerous emotional high that pushes him or her to more extreme behavior.

Children who are bullied have a higher absentee rate because the bullying makes them feel physically sick.

Bullying takes place anywhere children gather: the playground, the cafeteria, the school hallways, the school bus, the mall, online on websites such as MySpace, or on cell phones via calls and text messaging. Bullying takes the form of punching, hitting, tripping, name-calling, posting embarrassing messages or photographs, or sending nasty messages. Bullies can be boys or girls, known or unknown to their victims.

Who Are the Victims?

Children who are bullied are often singled out because they are seen as different; that is, nerdy, overweight, or too shy, of a different race or background, the new kid in school, or physically or mentally challenged. According to an essay by Karen Gouze, Ph.D., on the Children's Memorial Hospital website, even more damaging than physical assault is "indirect" or "relational" bullying that involves isolating the victim from the group by spreading false rumors about him or her, or ignoring him or her. This type of bullying has been intensified by the use of the Internet and it is more difficult for parents and teachers to spot. The WebMD site (www.webmd.com) reports that children who are bullied have a higher absentee rate because the bullying makes them feel physically sick, and they wanted to avoid going to school and encountering the bully.

April Himes of Poteau, Oklahoma, was a typical middle-school student. However, she had been singled out by her peers and teased because of her appearance. The teasing continued so long and so intensely that she committed suicide rather than go to school and face her tormentors one more day. On the memorial website posted by her parents, there is a gallery of seven other children from across the United States who were also bullied into the extreme response of suicide.

Bullying escalates the longer it goes unreported.

What Are the Warning Signs?

Parents are cautioned to watch for indications that their child has been bullied, such as:

- depression, feelings of worthlessness

- anxiety, nausea, fear of going to school

- sleeplessness, nightmares

- withdrawal from family, friends and activities that were always pleasurable.

However, Dr. Gouze also encourages pediatricians in particular to help parents "build children's resilience." From the time their children are preschoolers, parents should

- foster self-esteem in their children,

- teach them to respect others and interact . . . in socially acceptable ways,

- model how to respond assertively, but not aggressively, to negative comments,

- encourage them to buddy up with other children as a support system, and

- teach them to know when to tell an adult about negative behaviors that they experience or observe.

The final step is crucial because bullying escalates the longer it goes unreported, and no one steps in to stop the behavior. Delayed intervention hurts the bully as much as the child being bullied.

Who Are the Bullies?

Children may become bullies because they have been the victims of bullying. According to 2001 study by psychologist Tonja Nansel, Ph.D., 6% of the 15,000 U.S. sixth- through tenth-graders she surveyed responded that they had been both bullies and the victims of bullies. Bullies may be emotionally immature and insecure, and [they may] lack social skills and the ability to take responsibility for their actions or choices. According to www.kidshealth.org, if a bully continues his or her aggressive behavior past his or her late teens, he or she not only risks losing friends who now view such behavior as immature, but also risks becoming the one out of every four elementary school bullies [who] has a criminal record by the time he or she is thirty years old.

Episodes of school shootings have been linked to bullying, as former victims of bullying were so emotionally distressed that they resorted to an extreme and violent form of bullying as a response to the treatment they received. The Secret Service and the U.S. Department of Education investigated 37 school shootings across the country and discovered that 66% of student gunmen stated that they had been bullied.

Dylan Klebold and Eric Harris, the teenage gunmen who killed 12 students and a teacher and injured 23 others before killing themselves in the 1999 Columbine High School shootings, left writings detailing the bullying they felt led to their behavior. However, according to Jordan Peterson, a professor at the University of Toronto and a clinical psychologist, this type of extreme response is not the norm, but a result of someone who is "profoundly alienated." In his interview with CTV.ca News, Peterson stated that everyone experiences "hurt, loss, or rejection" in their lives, but most find non-violent ways to overcome those experiences.

What Are the Warning Signs?

Just as parents should watch for signs that their child has been the victim of a bully, parents should watch for signs that their child might be becoming a bully such as:

- Withdrawal from family, friends, and activities that were always pleasurable

- Feelings of worthlessness, friendlessness

- Physical or verbal aggression, i.e. pushing, hitting, or name-calling

- Lack of sympathy for a child who has been hurt or teased

- Lying

- Lack of contact with other children, such as fewer invitations to join classmates' parties or games, and

- Sudden possession of new toys, gadgets, or money that he or she bullied classmates into handing over

Some of the warning signs for bullies and their victims are similar, such as withdrawal from family and friends. The same methods of building "resilience" in a potential victim of bullying will work to help a child avoid becoming a bully. Helping a child find positive and acceptable ways to deal with anxiety, frustration, and anger can keep him or her from the emotional and social alienation that can deepen until the child lashes out in an extreme response.

Schools across the United States lack uniform and effective policies for dealing with and preventing bullying. Although parents should contact their child's teacher and school administration for help in dealing with bullying, parents are the best means of defense, and early intervention is crucial. Parents must learn to recognize the warning signs of their children being bullied or becoming bullies, take these signs seriously, and act to help their children find ways to deal with the problem. No child should be afraid to go to school or be so angry with his or her classmates that he or she targets them for harm or harassment.

15

Punishment Therapy Violates the Rights of Children with Disabilities

The Alliance to Prevent Restraint, Aversive Interventions, and Seclusion (APRAIS)

The Alliance to Prevent Restraint, Aversive Interventions, and Seclusion (APRAIS) was established in 2004 by leading education, research, and advocacy organizations to protect children with significant disabilities from abuse in schools, treatment programs, and residential facilities.

Every day, children with disabilities or challenging behaviors are routinely subjected to painful and traumatizing treatment by licensed caregivers. To make matters worse, these abusive treatments—such as hitting or punching a child, restraining a child so that he or she cannot move, or locking a child in a closet— have been shown to cause more harm than good, spawning children who feel helpless, frustrated, angry, or violent while the underlying cause goes undetected and unresolved. The use of such abusive techniques on children should be considered cruel and unusual punishment, thereby a violation of the Eighth Amendment to the United States Constitution.

Every day in this country, children with disabilities are needlessly being subjected to harmful practices in the name of treating "challenging behaviors." They are brought down to the ground and straddled, strapped or tied in chairs and beds, blindfolded slapped and pinched, startled by cold water sprays in the face, deprived of food, secluded in locked rooms, and more, despite the fact that research and practice show that these techniques exacerbate challenging behavior and do nothing to teach the child appropriate behaviors. . . .

The deliberate use of pain, humiliation, exclusion, and immobilization on a child has all the hallmarks of abuse.

Across the country, teachers, aides, and program staff who have been entrusted with children's care, protection, education, and development are subjecting them to this "treatment." In fact, such negative and dangerous activities are often inappropriately included as part of these children's education plans in the hope that they will reduce the occurrence of unwanted behavior. Children learn nothing about acceptable behavior from the experience of being hurt, secluded, or immobilized by their caregivers. Children with serious communication, social, and behavior challenges need effective, research-based, positive approaches based on Positive Behavior Supports (PBS). PBS teaches desired behaviors [and] useful skills, and fosters healthy emotional development and interactions with others. PBS is widely accepted as effective evidence-based practice that not only reduces even the most dangerous and disruptive behaviors, but focuses on the vision of quality of life.

Sanctioned Abuse

Many parents are unaware that their children are being routinely hurt, restrained, secluded, and subjected to painful and ineffective practices by their school or program. Some have signed vague or confusing consent forms which offered no clear picture of the dangerous interventions planned for their child. Other parents are aware of and deeply troubled by the methods used on their child, but have been threatened with loss of the placement or other essential services if they object.

The deliberate use of pain, humiliation, exclusion, and immobilization on a child has all the hallmarks of abuse. Most parents assume that a child with disabilities has the same protections against abuse that other children are given. Unfortunately, the programmatic application of these abusive procedures on children with disabilities is often treated differently. In many special education programs and service delivery systems the use of pain and humiliation (aversive interventions) and immobilization (restraint and seclusion) to control or change behavior is state-sanctioned—allowed under a confusing patchwork of outdated, poorly written, or overly permissive laws and regulations. When abuse is permitted in this way, parents may find that the usual responses to child endangerment, such as seeking help from school administrators, the police, or the courts, fail to solve the immediate threat their child is facing. When abuse is sanctioned, it becomes less visible. Injuries and deaths involving these procedures are believed to be significantly underreported. The kinds of investigations that would expose the nature and extent of the problem are seldom done, and accurate information based on medical or forensic reporting is difficult to obtain. The deaths and injuries of children with disabilities are too easily blamed on accidents or on aspects of the disability itself. But in recent years parents are speaking out, and advocacy organizations, legislators, and the courts are realizing the seriousness of this threat to the basic human rights of vulnerable children and youth.

Aversive interventions, restraint, and seclusion are used on children across the spectrum of disabilities, including those with autism, learning disabilities, mental health needs, cognitive challenges, and children with physical and sensory disabilities. Schools and programs continue to use aversive interventions, restraint, and seclusion for a variety of unacceptable reasons, for example: because they are understaffed; for staff convenience; because they think "bad behavior" should be punished; because they do not believe the children they serve have the same needs, rights, and feelings as children who do not have disability labels; or because the school or program lacks leadership and does not empower teachers and staff with the knowledge, support, and positive alternatives they need.

The use of aversives, restraint and seclusion has resulted in hundreds of deaths and thousands of injuries. Even when no physical harm is apparent, these techniques cause psychological trauma and rob people of their dignity.

Types of Abusive Treatment

Aversive interventions (or "aversives") involve the deliberate infliction of physical and/or emotional pain and suffering, for the purpose of changing or controlling a child's behavior. Aversives include (but are not limited to) techniques such as direct physical or corporal punishment (hitting or pinching); visual screening; forcing a child to inhale or ingest noxious substances; sensory deprivation; depriving a child of food, use of a toilet, or other health-sustaining necessities; and temporarily but significantly depriving a child of the ability to move. Use of restraint devices as well as blindfolds, visual screens, and white noise helmets results in sensory deprivation. Techniques that deliberately disrupt a child's basic emotional well-being and sense of safety, or that result in the long-term loss of the normal freedoms and pleasures of childhood by preventing exercise, peer interactions or other activities may also be considered aversive.

Restraint is a type of aversive that involves the forced restriction or immobilization of the child's body or parts of the body, contingent on a designated behavior. There are three types of restraint. Manual restraint involves various "holds" for grabbing and immobilizing a child or bringing a child to the floor. The child is kept in the chosen restraint position by one or more staff person's arms, legs, or body weight. Mechanical restraint is the use of straps, cuffs, mat and blanket wraps, helmets, and other devices to prevent movement and/or sense perception, often by pinning the child's limbs to a splint, wall, bed, chair, or floor. Chemical restraint means using medication to stop behavior by dulling a child's ability to move and/or think. Medication specifically prescribed to treat symptoms of a disability or illness is not a chemical restraint.

It is generally accepted that brief physical intervention used to interrupt an immediate and serious danger to the child or others may be called for in the case of safety emergency. This is different from the ongoing use of restraint as punishment or in the guise of treatment for a child's disability or behavior. Frequent use of emergency restraint is an indication [that] program revision is needed, even if the program is considered positive.

Seclusion involves forced isolation in a room or space from which the child cannot escape. Allowing a child to voluntarily take a break from activities is not considered seclusion.

A child who is squirted in the face each time he or she screams is not learning new and better ways to communicate.

Long-Term Behavioral Problems

Positive behavior interventions are safe in the short run, and in the long run promote habits and attitudes that continue to reduce risk. On the other hand, aversive interventions, restraint, and seclusion may cause injury and death, and they can backfire in ways that cannot be predicted or controlled. According to the professional literature, the following are some crucial considerations in choosing safe, respectful, and effective interventions:

• Children generalize what they learn. Anxiety and avoidance triggered by aversives, restraint, and seclusion will spread to other areas of a child's life and become an obstacle to achieving desirable behaviors, attitudes, and progress. For example, a child who experiences aversive procedures in the classroom will come to fear and avoid the classroom itself, the teacher, the school bus, the school, and the learning process in general.

• Children learn from their experiences with adults. Physically coercive activities teach children that "might makes right" and that physical means of problem-solving are acceptable. The small child who is easily restrained today will soon become a large, strong teenager able to demonstrate the dangerous behavior he/she has been taught.

• We can help a child best by seeking the underlying cause of his or her behavior. When aversive techniques, restraint, and seclusion are used to stop behavior for the short term, the real cause of that behavior goes undetected and unresolved. The underlying cause, whether medical, emotional, or social, is masked by these methods and can worsen as a result of the very techniques used.

• Adults can teach children alternate ways to communicate. Helping children learn new skills provides them with opportunities for achieving success. Aversive strategies, restraint, and seclusion do not offer [a] child useful alternative behaviors. For instance, a child who is squirted in the face each time he or she screams is not learning new and better ways to communicate with teachers and staff or to solve the problem that is causing the screams.

• Positive strategies can flourish only when negative interventions are rejected. The use of restraint, seclusion, and restrictive techniques take time, training, and imaginative energy away from the search for positive strategies for children with disabilities. Teachers or staff may be caught in a cycle of negative responses from which it becomes increasingly difficult to escape.

• Trusting relationships between a child and his or her teacher, combined with a sense of safety, are fundamental for healthy child development. Aversives, restraint, and seclusion eliminate the opportunity for such an environment or relationship.

• Children need to know that their bodies are their own, and that sometimes it is right to refuse or say "no." When children are taught that it is appropriate for adults to grab and hold them, and that a "good" child should submit without objection, these children can become easy victims for sexual predators.

• All children should enjoy equal protection from danger and risk. Children with disabilities are already three times more likely to be abused than children without disabilities. Permitting dangerous activities labeled as treatment leaves this vulnerable group with unequal protection under the law.

• When children with disabilities are taught alongside their typical peers, positive strategies are more likely to be the norm. Schools and programs that use aversives, restraint, and seclusion tend to operate in segregated settings, away from public view, because these dangerous interventions violate community standards and values.

Trauma and Child Development

Practitioners of aversive techniques, restraint, and seclusion used to believe that if the child was not physically injured by such interventions, they had done a safe job. Now we know better.

Advances in our understanding of child development emphasize the importance of a secure, well-balanced emotional life. A child repeatedly subjected to these techniques grows up feeling helpless, frightened, frustrated, or angry. The child's reactions may become increasingly stressed.

Over time, the overworked stress response system of the child's brain can become unbalanced, creating an ongoing state of high arousal. Repetitive, impulsive activity patterns, such as the "fight or flight" response, become locked in as the child's brain chemistry changes. The child becomes less able to control emotions, to pay attention, or to take in new information and use it to make appropriate decisions. Eventually, such a child may misinterpret even the well-intended actions of others as threatening.

These classic responses to trauma interrupt and can permanently alter brain development. They fuel a downward spiral in which teachers or program staff are both creating and responding to the child's anger and inflexibility.

No Justifiable Reasons

There are no justifiable reasons for using aversive interventions, restraint, and seclusion. Law and regulations covering most children's service delivery systems generally agree that aversive interventions, restraint, and seclusion may not be used for purposes of staff convenience, or as coercion, punishment, or retaliation. These methods are not "teaching" methods because they do not teach positive behaviors. The use of aversive interventions, restraint, and seclusion under the guise of therapeutic or educational interventions is unethical because these procedures create risk and unnecessarily take away basic rights. There is a lack of evidence that aversive techniques offer a safe means of teaching desirable, self-directed behavior that a child can maintain over the long term. Safe, positive methods of changing and redirecting behavior are well-documented. Evidence shows them to be successful regardless of the child's diagnostic label, degree of disability, or severity of behaviors. The responsibility to employ best practices and the obligation to do no harm in treatment require that the least dangerous, least intrusive, and least restrictive methods always be used.

Individual liberty is protected under the doctrine of least restrictive alternative (LRA). LRA requires careful consideration of the individual's interests; the purpose of treatment; and the interventions and environments chosen to provide treatment. Additionally, interventions must be demonstrated as effective for the purpose for which they are used, and there must be proof of therapeutic justification. LRA, therefore, provides parents and advocates a strong constitutionally based argument in favor of positive interventions over the use of aversive interventions, restraint, and seclusion—all highly restrictive procedures. . . .

The use of aversives, non-emergency restraint, and seclusion in facilities run by federal, state, or local governments raises important issues of constitutional protections. Some courts have ruled against the use of these behavioral interventions on people with disabilities on the grounds that [doing so violates] the Eighth Amendment prohibition against "cruel and unusual punishment." Other legal decisions have found the Eighth Amendment to apply only to prisons and other penal facilities. This leads to a seemingly indefensible predicament: certain aversives and restraints permitted for "therapeutic" use on children with disabilities are considered too inhumane to be constitutionally applied as punishments in prisons.

Unjustified restraint use in public facilities has been successfully challenged as a violation of constitutionally protected liberty interests under the Fourteenth Amendment. The Supreme Court (in *Youngberg v. Romeo*, 1982) found that a man with mental retardation who was committed to a state facility had constitutional rights, including a right to reasonably safe conditions of confinement, freedom from unreasonable bodily restraints, and minimally adequate training. The Supreme

Court thus adopted the position that persons involuntarily committed "retain liberty interests in freedom of movement and in personal security" and that providers risk liability when they use aversives or restraints.

16

Children's Rights Should Be Considered with Regard to Parenthood

Elizabeth Marquardt

Elizabeth Marquardt is the director of the Center for Marriage and Families at the Institute for American Values in New York and the author of Between Two Worlds: The Inner Lives of Children of Divorce.

A clash between adult rights and children's needs with regard to parenthood and conception is emerging throughout the world. With the advent of assisted reproductive technologies—for example, in vitro fertilization, DNA experimentation, and stem cell research for cloning—along with the already established practices of adoption and legal guardianship, governments and societies are altering the traditional definition of parenthood by using such terms as "natural parent," "legal parent," "psychological parent," or even "Progenitor A and Progenitor B." While all of this is going on, the fundamental rights and best interest of the children are becoming lost. More time and research should be devoted to understanding the needs of children before new laws change the time-honored definition of parenthood.

Around the world, the two-person, mother-father model of parenthood is being fundamentally challenged.

In Canada, with virtually no debate, the controversial law that brought about same-sex marriage quietly included the provision to erase the term "natural parent" across the board in federal law, replacing it with the term "legal parent." With that law, the locus of power in defining who a child's parents are shifts precipitously from civil society to the state, with the consequences as yet unknown.

In Spain, after the recent legalization of same-sex marriage, the legislature changed the birth certificates for all children in that nation to read "Progenitor A" and "Progenitor B" instead of "mother" and "father." With that change, the words "mother" and "father" were struck from the first document issued to every newborn by the state. Similar proposals have been made in other jurisdictions that have legalized same-sex marriage.

In New Zealand and Australia, influential law commissions have proposed allowing children conceived with use of sperm or egg donors to have three legal parents. Yet neither group addresses the real possibility that a child's three legal parents could break up and feud over the child's best interests.

Courts often must determine who the legal parents are among the many adults who might be involved in planning, conceiving, birthing, and raising a child.

In the United States, courts often must determine who the legal parents are among the many adults who might be involved in planning, conceiving, birthing, and raising a child. In a growing practice, judges in several states have seized upon the idea of "psychological" parenthood to award legal parent status to adults who are not related to children by blood, adoption, or marriage. At times they have done so even over the objection of the child's biological parent. Also, successes in the same-sex marriage debate have encouraged group marriage advocates who wish to break open the two-person understanding of marriage and parenthood.

Scientists Get Involved

Meanwhile, scientists around the world are experimenting with the DNA in eggs and sperm in nearly unimaginable ways, raising the specter of children born with one or three genetic parents, or two same-sex parents. Headlines recently announced research at leading universities in Britain and New Zealand that could enable same-sex couples or single people to procreate. In Britain, scientists were granted permission to create embryos with three genetic parents. Stem cell research has introduced the very real possibility that a cloned child could be born—and the man who pioneered in vitro fertilization (IVF) treatment has already said in public that cloning should be offered to childless couples who have exhausted other options. The list goes on.

Nearly all of these steps, and many more, are being taken in the name of adult rights to form families they choose. But what about the children? . . .

At stake are the most elemental features of children's well-being—their social and physical health and their moral and spiritual wholeness.

Questions Arise Concerning Adult Rights Versus Child Need

Right now, our societies urgently require reflection, debate, and research about the policies and practices that will serve the best interests of children—those already born and those yet to be born. This report argues that around the world the state is taking an increasingly active role in defining and regulating parenthood far beyond its limited, vital, historic, and child-centered role in finding suitable parents for needy children through adoption. The report documents how the state creates new uncertainties and vulnerabilities when it increasingly seeks to administer parenthood, often giving far greater attention to adult rights than to children's needs. For the most part, this report does not advocate for or against particular policy prescriptions (such as banning donor conception) but rather seeks to draw urgently needed public attention to the current revolutionary changes in parenthood, to point out the risks and contradictions arising from increased state intervention, and to insist that our societies immediately undertake a vigorous, child-centered debate.

Children have a right and need to know their origins.

Do mothers and fathers matter to children? Is there anything special—anything worth supporting—about the two-person, mother-father model? Are children commodities to be produced by the marketplace? What role should the state have in defining parenthood? When adult rights clash with children's needs, how should the conflict be resolved? These are the questions raised by this report. Our societies will either answer these questions democratically and as a result of intellectually and morally serious reflection and public debate, or we will find, very soon, that these questions have already been answered for us. The choice is ours. At stake are the most elemental features of children's well-being—their social and physical health and their moral and spiritual wholeness. . . .

Government Plays an Active Role in Defining Parenthood

At this moment, with virtually no public discussion, the relationship that is most core and vital to children's very survival—that of parenthood—is being fundamentally redrawn through new laws, proposals, and practices affecting marriage, reproduction, and family life, with the state playing an increasingly active role in defining parenthood for broader categories of children.

Given that in some ways the genie is already out of the bottle, it is not entirely clear what actions the state and social leaders should take in the near future. For instance, some nations have moved to ban the practice of anonymous donation of sperm and eggs. This would seem to be a positive development for children—after all, there is a strong argument to be made that children have a right and need to know their origins. Yet greater acceptance of the idea that donor-conceived children have a right to know their origins is also leading to the idea that these children should have the possibility of some kind of *relationship* with their sperm or egg donor (and not just a file of information), or even that the donor should have some kind of legal parental status in the child's life, . . . as in New Zealand and Australia, where commissions have proposed allowing donors to "opt in" as children's third legal parents.

What might the future hold for children with three or more legal parents? We have no idea.

Or, in another example, after Britain passed a law banning donor anonymity there was a purported drastic drop in the number of men willing to donate sperm. The state health service then began an active campaign to recruit sperm and egg donors, no longer just allowing the intentional conception of children who will not know or be raised in relationship with their own biological parents, but very intentionally promoting it. Meanwhile, couples in that nation who wish to conceive have even greater incentive to go abroad to nations or regions that have less regulation—such as Spain, India, Eastern Europe, or elsewhere—to procure sperm or eggs or surrogate wombs, making it even less likely that their child will ever be able to trace their origins or form a relationship with a distant donor abroad.

Again, how will these developments affect children? At the moment we have no real idea. But we certainty do have serious and immediate cause for concern.

Research About Children's Well-Being Is Necessary

For reasons like these, this report does not conclude with the usual list of specific policy recommendations. Rather, this report issues a call to fellow citizens in the United States and Canada and around the world. The call is for all of us to participate in urgently needed conversation and research about the revolution in parenthood and the needs of children.

When there is a clash between adult rights and children's needs, the children should take precedence.

This much is clear: When society changes marriage, it changes parenthood. The divorce revolution and the rise in single-parent childbearing weakened ties of fathers to their children and introduced a host of players at times called "parents." The use of assisted reproductive technologies by married heterosexual couples—and later by singles and same-sex couples—raised still more uncertainties about the meaning of motherhood and fatherhood and exposed children to new losses the adults never fathomed. The legalization of same-sex marriage, while sometimes seen as a small change affecting just a few people, raises the startling prospect of fundamentally breaking the legal institution of marriage from any ties to biological parenthood. Meanwhile, successes in the same-sex marriage debate have encouraged others who wish fully and completely to break open the two-person understanding of marriage and parenthood.

Here is where we are. In law and culture, the two-natural-parent, mother-father model is falling away, replaced with the idea that children are fine with any one or more adults being called their parents, so long as the appointed parents are nice people. This change is happening incrementally, largely led by self-appointed experts and advocates in a few fields. But it does not have to be this way. Those of us who are concerned can and should take up and lead a debate about the lives of children and the future of parenthood.

As we launch this conversation, a guiding principle could be this: When there is a clash between adult rights and children's needs, the interests of the more vulnerable party—in this case, the children—should take precedence. A great deal of evidence supports the idea that children, on average, do best when raised by their own, married mother and father, with adoption as an important, pro-child, admirable alternative. With regard to some newly visible family forms, such as families headed by gay or lesbian parents or those created using donor sperm, eggs, or surrogacy, we have more to learn more about the lasting, inner experience of the children.

To provide time and space for this conversation and for more research, this report also calls for a moratorium or a "time out" lasting five years. Until we better understand and prioritize the needs of children, no legislatures, courts, or commissions should press forward with recommendations or changes that broadly undermine the normative importance of mothers and fathers in the lives of children, nor should they support intentionally denying unborn children knowledge of and a relationship with their own mother and father. Rather, they should concentrate their energies on rigorous inquiry and active debate about the needs of children and the role of mothers and fathers in their lives.

The well-being of the world's children calls us to act—not years from now but right now. For their sake, for those born and those yet to be born, we must be willing to launch a sometimes uncomfortable but urgent debate about the well-being of children born in an age that is rapidly redefining the meaning of parenthood. Nothing is inevitable. The time to act is now.

Organizations to Contact

The editors have compiled the following list of organizations concerned with the issues debated in this book. The descriptions are derived from materials provided by the organizations. All have publications or information available for interested readers. The list was compiled on the date of publication of the present volume; the information provided here may change. Be aware that many organizations take several weeks or longer to respond to inquiries, so allow as much time as possible.

Advocates for Youth
2000 M Street NW, Suite 750, Washington, DC   20036
(202) 419-3420 • fax: (202) 419-1448
e-mail: information@advocatesforyouth.org
Web site: www.advocatesforyouth.org

Advocates for Youth believes young people have the right to accurate and complete sexual health information to enable them to make healthy decisions about sexuality, and about confidential reproductive and sexual health services. The organization publishes fact sheets and brochures on adolescent behavior and sexuality including "Comprehensive Sex Education: Research and Results" and "Science and Success: Clinical Services and Contraceptive Access."

American Civil Liberties Union (ACLU)
125 Broad Street, 18th Floor, New York, NY   10004-2400
(212) 54-2500
e-mail: infoaclu@aclu.org
Web site: www.aclu.org

The ACLU is a national organization that works to defend Americans' civil rights guaranteed by the U.S. Constitution. Seeking to protect the rights of students and others, it opposes random school searches and drug testing, zero tolerance

policies, racism, sexism, homophobia, and religious intoler-
ance. The ACLU offers policy statements and pamphlets, and
its *Blog of Rights* discusses many topics including reproductive
freedom, and youth and schools.

Child Labor Coalition (CLC)

1701 K Street NW, Suite 1200, Washington, DC   20006
(202) 835-3323 • fax: (202) 835-0747
e-mail: childlabor@nclnet.org
Web site: stopchildlabor.org

The CLC, a group of more than twenty organizations, repre-
sents consumers, labor unions, educators, human rights and
labor rights groups, child advocacy groups, and religious and
women's groups. It was established in 1989 and is cochaired
by the National Consumers League and the American Federa-
tion of Teachers. Its mission is to protect working youth and
to promote legislation, programs, and initiatives to end child
labor exploitation in the United States and abroad. The CLC's
Web site offers news reports, press releases, and fact sheets, including "Children in the Fields: The Inequitable Treatment of
Child Farmworkers" and "Youth Peddling Crews: Sweatshops
of the Streets."

Children's Rights Information Network (CRIN)

East Studio, 2 Pontypool Place, London   SE1 8QF
   United Kingdom
+44-20-7401-2257
e-mail: info@crin.org
Web site: www.crin.org

CRIN is an international network of children's rights organizations that supports the effective exchange of information
about children and their rights to help implement the United
Nations Convention on the Rights of the Child. The network
publishes information on children's rights, including "Children and Adolescents Statement: Strategies for International
Cooperation" and "Haiti: Lost Childhoods in Haiti."

Child Trends

4301 Connecticut Ave. NW, Suite 350, Washington, DC 20008

(202) 572-6000 • fax: (202) 362-8420

Web site: www.childtrends.org

Child Trends is a nonprofit, nonpartisan research center that studies children at all stages of development. The organization works to improve outcomes for children by providing research, data, and analysis to the people and institutions whose decisions and actions affect children, including program providers, the policy community, researchers and educators, and the media. Founded in 1979, Child Trends helps keep the nation focused on children and their needs by identifying emerging issues; evaluating important programs and policies; and providing data-driven, evidence-based guidance on policy and practice. In addition to the newsletter *Facts at a Glance*, which presents the latest data on sexual behavior and teen pregnancy for cities and states, and the periodic newsletter *The Child Indicator*, CT also publishes fact sheets, including *Contraceptive Use Patterns Across Teens' Sexual Relationships* and *Neighborhood Support and Children's Connectedness*.

Committee on the Rights of the Child (CRC)

Office of the United Nations High Commissioner
for Human Rights, Palais des Nations
Geneva 10 CH-1211
Switzerland
+41 22-928-92-24 • fax: +41 22-928-90-10
Web site: www2.ohchr.org/english/bodies/crc

The CRC is a body of independent experts that monitors implementation of the United Nations Convention on the Rights of the Child by governments that have ratified the convention. The committee is made up of eighteen members from different countries who are considered to be experts in the field of human rights. The CRC publishes sessional and annual reports, press releases, and meeting summaries.

Education World

1062 Barnes Road, Suite 301, Wallingford, CT   06492
e-mail: webmaster@educationworld.com
Web site: www.educationworld.com

Education World is a site where teachers and administrators share ideas, find research materials, and read daily columns. Educators can browse hundreds of articles written by education experts covering such topics as dress codes, drug education, and school safety. The organization prints twelve newsletters, including *Weekly Newsletter: What's New This Week?* and *Headlines Newsletter.*

Freechild Project

PO Box 6185, Olympia, WA   98507-6185
(360) 489-9680
e-mail: info@freechild.org
Web site: www.freechild.org

The Freechild Project is a think tank, resource agency, and advocacy group for young people around the world who seek to play a larger role in their schools and communities. Training and conferences are offered to help parents, teachers, and community leaders involve youth in their communities. The Freechild Project publishes booklets, fact sheets, speeches, and book reviews, and its resources directory offers a wealth of information about school uniforms, zero tolerance, free speech, and student equality.

Human Rights Watch

350 Fifth Ave., New York, NY   10118-3299
(212) 290-4700 • fax: (212) 736-1300
e-mail: hrwnyc@hrw.org
Web site: www.hrw.org

Human Rights Watch is an activist organization dedicated to protecting the human rights of people around the world, including workers' rights. It investigates and exposes human rights violations and holds abusers accountable. It publishes an annual world report, and in its Children's Rights section has published "U.S.: Adopt Stronger Laws for Child Farmworkers" and "Indonesia: Protect Child Domestic Workers."

National Labor Committee (NLC)
5 Gateway Center, 6th Floor, Pittsburgh, PA 15222
(412) 562-2406 • fax: (412) 562-2411
e-mail: nlc@nlcnet.org
Web site: www.nlcnet.org

The committee seeks to educate and actively engage the U.S. public on human and labor rights abuses by corporations. Through education and activism, it works to end labor and human rights violations, ensure a living wage, and help workers and their families live and work with dignity. It produces videos, posters, and reports, including "Broken Lives: Behind U.S. Production in China," and "Child Labor Is Back."

Save the Children
54 Wilton Road, Westport, CT 06880
(800) 728-3843
Web site: www.savethechildren.org

Save the Children is an independent organization that seeks to ensure every child's right to survival, protection, education, and health. The organization publishes newsletters, research reports, issue briefs, fact sheets, and policy reports, including "Rewrite the Future: Education for Children in Conflict-Affected Countries."

Students for Sensible Drug Policy (SSDP)
1623 Connecticut Ave. NW, Suite 300, Washington, DC 20009
(202) 293-4414 • fax: (202) 293-8344
e-mail: ssdp@ssdp.org
Web site: www.ssdp.org

Students for Sensible Drug Policy is an international grassroots network of students who are concerned about the impact drug abuse has on communities, but who also know that the War on Drugs is failing. SSDP mobilizes and empowers young people to participate in the political process, pushing for sensible policies to achieve a safer and more just future, while fighting back against counterproductive Drug War policies, particularly ones that directly harm students and youth. SSDP prints pamphlets and flyers to encourage others to oppose drug testing in schools and to help change drug policies at the campus level.

United Nations Children's Fund (UNICEF)

UNICEF House, 3 United Nations Plaza, New York, NY 10017
(212) 686-5222 • fax: (212) 779-1679
e-mail: information@unicefusa.org
Web site: www.unicef.org

UNICEF, a nonpartisan organization, is mandated by the United Nations General Assembly to advocate for the protection of children's rights and to expand their opportunities. UNICEF upholds the Convention on the Rights of the Child and provides health care, clean water, improved nutrition, and education to millions of children worldwide. Among its publications are the yearly reports "The State of the World's Children," "Progress for Children," and the Annual Report, which spotlights significant results achieved on behalf of children around the world.

Bibliography

Books

Priscilla Alderson *Young Children's Rights: Exploring Beliefs, Principles and Practice, 2nd Edition.* Philadelphia, PA: Jessica Kingsley Publishers, 2008.

Barbara Coloroso *The Bully, the Bullied, and the Bystander: From Preschool to High School—How Parents and Teachers Can Help Break the Cycle.* New York: Harper Paperbacks, 2009.

Foundation Intervida *Exploited Lives: Child Labor Exploitation.* Barcelona, Spain: Intervida.org, 2008.

Michael D.A. Freeman *Children's Health and Children's Rights.* Boston: Nijoff Publishers, 2006.

James Garbarino and Ellen de Lara *And Words Can Hurt Forever: How to Protect Adolescents from Bullying, Harassment and Emotional Violence.* New York: Free Press, 2003.

Martin Guggenheim *What's Wrong with Children's Rights.* Cambridge, MA: Harvard University Press, 2005.

Wendy Herumin *Child Labor Today: A Human Rights Issue.* Berkeley Heights, NJ: Enslow Publishers, 2008.

Abigail Jones and   *Restless Virgins: Love, Sex, and*
Marissa Miley   *Survival at a New England Prep*
                     School. New York: HarperCollins,
                     2007.

Grace Ketterman   *Teaching Your Child About Sex: An*
                     Essential Guide for Parents. Grand
                     Rapids, MI: Revell, 2007.

Kathiann M.   *The Earls Case and the Student Drug*
Kowalski   *Testing Debate: Debating Supreme*
                     Court Decisions. Berkeley Heights, NJ:
                     Enslow Publishers, 2006.

Nicholas D.   *Half the Sky: Turning Oppression into*
Kristof and Sheryl   *Opportunity for Women Worldwide.*
WuDunn   New York: Alfred A. Knopf, 2009.

Bill O'Reilly and   *Kids Are Americans Too.* New York:
Charles Flowers   William Morrow, 2007.

John T. Pardeck   *Children's Rights: Policy and Practice.*
                     New York: Haworth Social Work
                     Practice Press, 2006.

Helena Silverstein   *Girls on the Stand: How Courts Fail*
                     Pregnant Minors. New York: New
                     York University Press, 2007.

Rosemarie Skaine   *Female Genital Mutilation: Legal,*
                     Cultural and Medical Issues. Jefferson,
                     NC: McFarland & Company, 2005.

Monica Feria   *The Landmark Rulings of the*
Tinta   *Inter-American Court of Human*
                     Rights on the Rights of the Child:
                     Protecting the Most Vulnerable at the
                     Edge. Boston: Nijoff Publishers, 2008.

Jonathan Todres, Mark E. Wojcik, Cris R. Revaz *The U.N. Convention on the Rights of the Child: An Analysis of Treaty Provisions and Implications of U.S. Ratification.* Ardsley, NY: Transnational Publishers, 2006.

Michael Wessells *Child Soldiers: From Violence to Protection.* Cambridge, MA: Harvard University Press, 2007.

Barbara Bennett Woodhouse *Hidden in Plain Sight: The Tragedy of Children's Rights from Ben Franklin to Lionel Tate.* Princeton, NJ: Princeton University Press, 2008.

Periodicals

Kat Aaron "Minors Fight for the Right to Vote," *American Observer*, October 16, 2008.

Associated Press "Rise in Bullying Has School Staffs in the Hot Seat: Most Not Trained to Handle It, Expert Says," March 31, 2010.

Zoe Chafe "Child Labor Harms Many Young Lives," WorldWatch.org, November 8, 2007.

Mona Charen "Yes, Abstinence Education: It's Still a Good Idea," *National Review*, September 3, 2008.

Victoria Clayton "Parents, Experts Divided on School Drug Testing," MSNBC.com, September 21, 2007.

E.R. Clough   "A Heartbreaking Visit to Child Labor Sweatshops," World of Good Development Organization, June 28, 2007, WorldofGood.org.

Michael C. Dorf   "What Constitutional Rights Should Schoolchildren Have? Two Recent Cases Underscore the Ways in Which Children Are Not Simply Miniature Adults," Findlaw.com, March 23, 2009.

Nancy Gibbs   "Birth Control for Kids?" *Time*, October 18, 2007.

Ryan Grim   "Blowing Smoke: Why Random Drug Testing Doesn't Reduce Student Drug Use," Slate.com, March 21, 2006.

Jennifer Haberkorn and S.A. Miller   "GAO Details Abuse Cases in Schools," *Washington Times*, May 20, 2009.

Benjamin Hess   "Children in the Fields: An American Problem," Association of Farmworker Opportunity Programs, May 2007.

Jesse J. Holland   "Savana Redding Strip Search Was Illegal, Supreme Court Says," *Huffington Post*, June 25, 2009.

Valerie Huber   "Opposing View: Best Message Is Abstinence," *USA Today*, September 3, 2008.

Hilary Hylton   "Texas Eases 'Zero Tolerance' Laws," *Time*, October 5, 2009.

Aaron Igdalsky   "Middle School Birth Control Is Absurd," *Daily Campus*, October 23, 2007.

Steph Kenrose   "The Case for Comprehensive Sex Education in Schools," Associated Content, July 29, 2009.

Jennifer Kern   "Drug Testing Students Counterproductive," *Seattle PI*, January 15, 2008.

Deborah Kotz   "A Debate About Teaching Abstinence," *US News & World Report*, December 19, 2007.

Tony Leys   "Uganda: Healing Former Child Soldiers," *Des Moines Register*, February 14, 2010.

Lindsay Lyon   "7 Reasons Parents Should Not Test Kids for Drug Use," *US News & World Report*, August 6, 2008.

Claire Morgenstern   "Ten Things You Should Know About Sex Education," Causecast.org, 2009.

Carolyn Moynihan   "Adults Still Trample Children's Rights: Abusive Institutions Have Closed Where Children Were Mistreated but Adults Still Abuse Children," *Spero News*, June 28, 2009.

Bill Muehlenberg   "Adult Selfishness, Child Suffering," BillMuehlenberg.com, July 16, 2009.

National Institute on Drug Abuse
"Frequently Asked Questions About Drug Testing in Schools," DrugAbuse.gov, September 2007.

Diana Philip
"Parental Involvement Laws: Why We Should Still Care That They Don't Work," Reproductive Health Reality Check, July 27, 2009, RHRealityCheck.org.

Luke Pryor
"In Defense of Sweatshops," *Cornell Daily Sun*, October 27, 2009.

Anna Quindlen
"Let's Talk About Sex," *Newsweek*, March 7, 2009.

Jennifer Riley
"Study: Abstinence Education Reduces Sexual Activity," *Christian Post*, February 3, 2010.

Mallory Simon
"My Bullied Son's Last Day on Earth," CNN.com, April 24, 2009.

Eileen Smolyar
"Lamb Chop, Sexual Education, and Birth Control Don't Go Together," *The Justice*, November 6, 2007.

Laura Sessions Stepp
"Study Casts Doubt on Abstinence-Only Programs," *Washington Post*, April 14, 2007.

Lindsay Tanner
"Study: Abstinence Program Might Work," Associated Press, February 2, 2010.

Ceil Than
"Facing the Bully in the Computer: What Is Cyberbullying?" Children's Rights of New York, Inc. *HOTLINE*, Vol. 29, No. 1, page 4, Spring 2008.

Ceil Than "Mean Girls Have Two Faces: How to Recognize Girl-to-Girl Bullying," Children's Rights of New York, Inc. *HOTLINE*, Vol. 29, No. 1, page 7, Spring 2008.

Dan K. Thomasson "One Justice Failed to See the Obvious," *San Diego Union Tribune*, July 9, 2009.

Greg Toppo "Restraint Can Dispirit and Hurt Special-Ed Students," *USA Today*, May 18, 2009.

United Nations Children's Fund "Female Genital Mutilation/Cutting: A Statistical Exploration," November 2005.

Ian Urbina "It's a Fork, It's a Spoon, It's a . . . Weapon?" *New York Times*, October 11, 2009.

Rebecca Webber, J. Scott Orr, and Brooke Lea Foster "Should Schools Use Restraints on Students?" *Parade Magazine*, July 26, 2009.

Elizabeth Weil "Teaching Boys and Girls Separately," *New York Times*, March 2, 2008.

Tiffany Ranae Widdifield "Should Kids in Middle School Have Access to Birth Control? Only If You Consider Yourself a Responsible Parent," Associated Content, October 18, 2007.

Michael Winerip "Drawing the Line on Drug Testing," *New York Times*, November 19, 2008.

Index

BOUNDARIES IN MARRIAGE

WORKBOOK

Resources by Henry Cloud and John Townsend

Books
Boundaries (and workbook)
Boundaries in Dating (and workbook)
Boundaries in Marriage (and workbook)
Boundaries with Kids (and workbook)
Boundaries with Teens (Townsend)
Changes That Heal (and workbook) (Cloud)
Hiding from Love (Townsend)
How People Grow (and workbook)
How to Have That Difficult Conversation You've Been Avoiding
Making Small Groups Work
The Mom Factor (and workbook)
Raising Great Kids
Raising Great Kids Workbook for Parents of Preschoolers
Raising Great Kids Workbook for Parents of School-Age Children
Raising Great Kids Workbook for Parents of Teenagers
Safe People (and workbook)
12 "Christian" Beliefs That Can Drive You Crazy

Video Curriculum
Boundaries
Boundaries in Dating
Boundaries in Marriage
Boundaries with Kids
Raising Great Kids for Parents of Preschoolers
ReGroup (with Bill Donahue)

Audio
Boundaries
Boundaries in Dating
Boundaries in Marriage
Boundaries with Kids
Boundaries with Teens (Townsend)
Changes That Heal (Cloud)
How People Grow
How to Have That Difficult Conversation You've Been Avoiding
Making Small Groups Work
The Mom Factor
Raising Great Kids

BOUNDARIES
IN MARRIAGE
WORKBOOK

UNDERSTANDING
THE CHOICES
THAT MAKE OR BREAK
LOVING RELATIONSHIPS

DR. HENRY CLOUD & DR. JOHN TOWNSEND

WITH LISA GUEST

ZONDERVAN®

ZONDERVAN.com/
AUTHORTRACKER
follow your favorite authors

We want to hear from you. Please send your comments about this book to us in care of zreview@zondervan.com. Thank you.

ZONDERVAN

Boundaries in Marriage Workbook
Copyright © 2000 by Henry Cloud and John Townsend

Requests for information should be addressed to:

Zondervan, *Grand Rapids, Michigan 49530*

ISBN 978-0-310-22875-2

Published in association with Yates & Yates, www.yates2.com.

Interior design by Laura Blost

Printed in the United States of America

Contents

Part Three—Resolving Conflict in Marriage

Part Four—Misunderstanding Boundaries in Marriage

How to Use This Workbook

*T*he *Boundaries in Marriage Workbook* can be used in a variety of ways.

- You will get the most out of your investment of time and energy if you are reading *Boundaries in Marriage* as you work through this book. The text fleshes out key concepts with real-life examples and a more thorough discussion of important points.
- You or, ideally, you and your spouse can use this workbook on your own. In tandem with the text, the questions in this workbook will help you become more aware of how healthy boundaries keep love alive and growing.
- You, or you and your spouse, can be part of a small group that meets regularly to discuss the challenges you face in your marriage and to pray for each other and your marriage.
- You might also work through this book with a prayer partner or accountability partner.
- Another option, with the approval of your therapist, is to use this workbook as an aid to structured individual or marital therapy.
- Whether you are working through *Boundaries in Marriage* on your own, with your spouse, or in a group, be sure to include plenty of prayer time. After all, God created marriage and, by his Spirit, empowers us to experience all that he intends for us.

May God bless you as, with his guidance, you establish boundaries that preserve and enhance your marriage and deepen your love for your spouse.

Lord God,

I'm a bit nervous as I set out on this journey toward a healthier marriage, and I'm feeling more than a little vulnerable. I know that you will be with me each step of the way, and may your presence give me hope and the willingness to proceed. And, as I submit myself to your transforming touch, I ask you to be at work in my mate even as you work to make me more like Christ—in whose name I pray. Amen.

A Tale of Two Couples

If you are reading this book, most likely marriage is important to you. You may be happy in your marriage and want to keep it growing. You may be struggling and dealing with major or minor problems. You may be single and want to prepare for marriage. You may be divorced and want to prevent the pain you went through if you remarry.

- Why are you reading this book? What do you hope to learn?

- How did you react when you read about the interaction between Harold and Sarah? What were your thoughts and feelings?

- How did you react to the picture of Frank and Julia's marriage? Again, what were your thoughts and feelings?

- If you are currently married, are you and your spouse building a marriage like Harold and Sarah's or like Frank and Julia's? Offer evidence to support your answer.

Both couples you met in the introduction were reaping the results of how they had conducted themselves in the earlier seasons of marriage. The first couple harvested a sad result; the other, a joyous one. It's our hope that this book will help you improve your harvest.

Your Life Begins Today (page 9)*

Most of us have no greater desire and prayer than a lifetime of love and commitment to one person with whom we can share life. Marriage is one of God's greatest gifts to humanity. It is the mystery of living as one flesh with another human being (Ephesians 5:31–32).

Marriage is first and foremost about love. It is bound together by the care, need, companionship, and values of two people, which can overcome hurt, immaturity, and selfishness to form something better than what each person alone can produce. Love is at the heart of marriage, as it is at the heart of God himself (1 John 4:16).

- When, in your own marriage or in a marriage you respect and admire, have you seen love overcome hurt, immaturity, or selfishness? Give a specific example.

- When have you seen or perhaps even experienced the partnership of marriage being "something better than what each person alone can produce"? Again, give a specific example.

Although love is at the heart of marriage, it is not enough. The marriage relationship needs other ingredients to grow and thrive. These ingredients are freedom and responsibility.

---

*The parts in italics are passages from the book *Boundaries in Marriage*. Page references to *Boundaries in Marriage* are in parentheses.

- When two people are free to disagree, they are free to love. When they are not free, they live in fear, and love is damaged.

    — Why does genuine love allow the freedom to disagree?

    — What fears come into play when people are not free to disagree—and why do those fears cause love to die?

- When two people together take responsibility to do what is best for the marriage, love can grow. When they do not, one takes on too much responsibility and resents it; the other does not take on enough and becomes self-centered or controlling.

    — What, if anything, do you see about yourself and/or your marriage when you look through the lens of the preceding statement?

Boundaries in Marriage is fundamentally about love. It is about promoting it, growing it, developing it, and repairing it. We want to help you develop love through providing a better environment for it: one of freedom and responsibility. This is where boundaries, or personal property lines, come in. They promote love by protecting individuals.

- Character is key. When people grow in character, they grow in the ability to set and receive boundaries in their marriages, and they mature. When they resist hearing the word *no*, they remain immature.

  — How do you define *character*?

  — At this point of your study, do your best to explain the connection between character and boundaries.

  — Think of toddlers you know. Why does resistance to the word *no* keep a person from maturing?

- Today is the day to work on your own boundaries in marriage. The issues you take initiative to deal with today will affect the rest of your married life. And the issues you ignore or are afraid to address will do the same.

  — Why do people choose to ignore issues in their marriage?

— What fears keep people from addressing issues in their marriage?

— What issues in your marriage do you need to be dealing with? Put differently, what issues are you choosing to ignore or what are you afraid to address?

You're headed toward either a Harold and Sarah marriage (they're still dealing immaturely with old, old boundary issues) or a Frank and Julia one (they've resolved boundary issues and have gone to much deeper stages of love and maturity), and you're doing that right now.

An Overview (page 11)

• Review the outline of *Boundaries in Marriage*.

— What section do you most look forward to reading? Why?

— What hope or excitement does this overview kindle?

Clarifying a Misconception (page 11)

• We need to make clear that *Boundaries in Marriage* is not about fixing, changing, or punishing your mate. If you aren't in control of yourself, the solution is not learning to control someone else. The solution is learning self-control.

— Be honest with yourself. What would you like to fix or change in your spouse or punish him/her for? Let go of those unhealthy and unhelpful goals by making them a topic of prayer; confess these desires and ask God to be at work in your mate even as he works to transform you.

— What aspects of your role as husband or wife currently call for you to exercise greater self-control? Again, submit those to the Lord and his sanctifying, transforming touch.

Boundaries in Marriage *is about taking ownership of your own life so that you are protected and you can love and protect your spouse without enabling or rescuing him or her.*

So, again, welcome to *Boundaries in Marriage*! We hope this is a helpful resource for you, whatever condition your marriage is in. We pray that as you learn to make the word *no* a good word in your marriage, responsibility and freedom will then help love take deep roots in both of your hearts. God bless you.

HENRY CLOUD, PH.D.
JOHN TOWNSEND, PH.D.

Part One

Understanding Boundaries

Chapter 1

What's a Boundary, Anyway?

*A*s she sat in front of the fireplace after Steve had gone to bed, Stephanie realized that their relationship was more "for him" than it was "for them," or even "for her." Get a grip, *she told herself.* Love is filled with sacrifice. But as much as she tried to see herself sacrificing for love, she felt as if she were sacrificing a lot, yet experiencing very little love.

The Importance of Boundaries (page 16)

The issues vary, but many people share Stephanie's perplexity. One spouse feels something is missing, but she can't figure out what it is. She gives, sacrifices, honors the commitment, and believes the best. And yet she does not resolve the pain she is in, nor does she achieve intimacy.

- Maybe you identify with Stephanie's situation. What experiences and conversations with your spouse have led to this point in your marriage?

- Perhaps a problem such as irresponsibility, a control issue, or even an addiction or abuse has seemed the reason for a lack of intimacy in your marriage. Why doesn't (or wouldn't) the resolution of this problem mean instant connection and renewed love?

- Why do you think a marriage commitment can be strong, but love, intimacy, and deep sharing not be present in the relationship?

- In the simplest sense, a boundary is a property line. It denotes the beginning and end of something. Why do boundaries encourage the development of intimacy and the growth of mates as individuals and as a couple?

Ownership (page 18)

In relationships, ownership is very important. If I know where the boundaries are in our relationship, I know who "owns" things such as feelings, attitudes, and behaviors. I know whom they "belong" to. And if there is a problem with one of those, I know to whom the problem belongs as well. A relationship like marriage requires each partner to have a sense of ownership of himself or herself.

- Remember Caroline and Joe? Each of them answered the question "Why do you . . . ?" with something about the other person. Neither one ever took personal ownership of his or her behavior. In their minds, their behavior was literally "caused" by the other person—a behavior dating back to the Garden of Eden.

  — What could Caroline have said to show ownership of her behavior rather than pointing to Joe's anger?

— What could Joe have said to own his behavior rather than pointing to Caroline's nagging and controlling?

— Think about a current problem in your marriage. What can you do to take ownership rather than blaming your spouse? If you haven't already, state the problem in such a way as to reflect your ownership of it.

The first way in which clarifying boundaries helps us is to know where one person ends and the other begins. What is the problem, and where is it? Is it in you, or is it in me?

Responsibility (page 20)

Boundaries help us to determine who is responsible for what. If we understand who owns what, we then know who must take responsibility for it. If Dr. Cloud could get Joe to see that his reactions were his problem and not Caroline's, then he could help Joe to take responsibility for changing his reactions.

- If we can see that the problem is our problem and that we are responsible for it, then we are in the driver's seat of change. So consider again the problem you identified in response to the previous question. What specific action did you find a sense of power for when you looked at the problem from the perspective of owning it?

Responsibility also involves action. We must actively participate in the resolution of whatever relational problem we might have, even if it is not our fault.

- Each spouse must take responsibility for the following things:

Feelings	Desires
Attitudes	Thoughts
Behaviors	Values
Choices	Talents
Limits	Love

— Explain the connection between *feelings* and *attitudes* and *behaviors.*

— What choice do you have about the feelings and attitudes that are behind the problem you have been considering?

— Look closely at the list above. In what areas are you not taking responsibility? (Could a close friend help you answer this question? Would your spouse be able to answer it if you risked asking an opinion?) What would responsibility in those areas look like? How might taking responsibility impact and improve your marriage?

We are not at the mercy of our spouse's behavior or problems. Each spouse can act both to avoid being a victim of the other spouse's problems and, better yet, to change the marriage relationship itself. Later in this book we will show you how to change your marriage for the better, even if your spouse is not interested in changing. But the process always begins with taking responsibility for your own part in the problem.

Freedom (page 22)

Remember Jen? She did not experience herself as a free agent. It never occurred to her that she had the freedom to respond, to make choices, to limit the ways her husband's behavior affected her. She felt that she was a victim of whatever he did or did not do.

- Imagine feeling like a victim of whatever your partner did or did not do. Give a specific example (hypothetical or real-life, your experience or someone else's) and then a specific suggestion or two about how you could limit the ways that behavior affected you.

- God designed us to have freedom of choice as we respond to life, to other people, to God, and to ourselves. But when we turned from God, we lost our freedom. Nevertheless, God tells us to not be subject to any kind of enslaving control at all (Galatians 5:1). Boundaries help us to realize our freedom once again.

  — Just as your next-door neighbor can't force you to paint your house purple, neither can any other human being make you do anything. What, if anything, do you feel your spouse is "making" you do?

  — At this point in your study of boundaries, what options for realizing your freedom from the enslavement you feel do you see for yourself?

- For love to work, each spouse has to realize his or her freedom. And boundaries help define the freedom we have and the freedom we do not have.

  — What freedom in a marriage helps foster love?

  — What lack of freedom (what limits or boundaries) helps foster love?

  — Consider the freedom you feel you do and do not have in your marriage. How might your marriage benefit from a clearer understanding—and more definite living out—of your freedom?

Marriage is based on a love relationship deeply rooted in freedom. Each partner is free from *the other and therefore free* to love *the other. Where there is control, or perception of control, there is not love. Love only exists where there is freedom.*

The Triangle of Boundaries (page 24)

Three realities have existed since the beginning of time: freedom, responsibility, and love. God created us free. He gave us responsibility for our freedom. And as responsible free agents, we are told to love him and each other. Something incredible happens as these three ingredients of relationship work together.

- As love grows, spouses become more free from the things that enslave: self-centeredness, sinful patterns, past hurts, and other self-imposed limitations. Then they gain a greater and greater sense of self-control and responsibility. As they act more responsibly, they become more loving. And then the cycle begins all over again.

  — When, if ever, have you seen this cycle working in a marriage or, ideally, experienced something of this cycle in your own marriage? Put differently, when has love given greater freedom from enslavement? When has greater responsibility made you or someone you know able to be more loving? Be as specific as possible about where you see this three-part cycle working, or—perhaps easier to see—not working.

  — Do you know any married person who could say that he or she has become more free to be oneself as a result of being loved in that relationship? If so, talk with that person to learn something about being a catalyst of growth for your spouse or about taking responsibility for yourself because of the way you're being loved.

  — The three legs of the triangle work when spouses are free to not react to the other, they take responsibility for their own issues, and they love the other person even when he or she does not deserve it. Free from each other, they give love to each other freely, and that love transforms and produces growth. Which leg of the triangle can you start to strengthen today? Be specific about what you will do toward that goal.

Love can only exist where freedom and responsibility are operating. Love creates more freedom that leads to more responsibility, which leads to more and more ability to love.

Protection (page 26)

The last aspect of boundaries that makes love grow is protection. You need protective boundaries that you can put up when evil is present and can let down when the danger is over. Boundaries need to keep the bad out and allow the good in.

- Remember Regina and Lee? What bad did Regina's boundaries need to keep out?

- What bad in a marriage you know needs to be kept out by boundaries? What about that situation makes maintaining boundaries difficult?

As it is with your house, so it is with your soul. You need protective boundaries that you can put up when evil is present and can let down when the danger is over.

Self-Control (page 28)

Boundaries are not selfish, nor are they to be used to be selfish. Boundaries are basically about self-control. Boundaries are not something you "set on" another person. Boundaries are about yourself.

- What boundaries have you tried to "set on" your spouse?

- In those situations, what boundaries, in the true sense of the term, could you set for yourself? Those boundaries may be consequences: how will you respond when your spouse behaves inappropriately?

If someone trespasses your personal boundaries in some way, you can take control of yourself and not allow yourself to be controlled or hurt anymore. This is self-control. And ultimately, self-control serves love, not selfishness.

Examples of Boundaries (page 29)

In the physical world, boundaries such as fences, doors, and locks define property and protect it. In the immaterial world of souls and relationships, boundaries are different. Let's look at some.

- **Words**—The most basic boundary is language. Your words help define you. They tell the other person who you are, what you believe, what you want, and what you don't want.

  — Give an example of boundary-setting words that you and your mate use occasionally, if not regularly.

  — How do you respond when your spouse uses boundary-setting words?

  — How does your spouse respond to your boundary-setting words?

— When have you—perhaps like Stephanie—chosen silence rather than boundary-setting words? Be specific.

• ***Truth***—God's truth and principles provide the boundaries of our existence, and as we live within this truth, we are safe. In addition, being honest and truthful about ourselves and what is going on in a relationship provides boundaries.

— Which of God's truth and principles are you especially aware of functioning well in your marriage? (Some are listed on page 30 of the text.) Which, if any, have been violated? What have been the consequences of that violation—and what might be done to get those boundaries back in place?

— When, if ever, have you been aware of giving your mate a false impression of your feelings or your perspective on the relationship? Why did you choose to do so? What have been the consequences of your choice?

- **Consequences**—Consequences define the boundary of what you will allow yourself to be exposed to (see page 31). When words fail to communicate, actions can.

  — When have the consequences of pain or loss helped you or your spouse better understand the other's boundaries?

  — In what current situation, if any, might the use of consequences be an effective communicator of your boundaries? What would those consequences be?

- **Emotional Distance**—A pure heart and the commitment to work on things are necessary as one follows the advice of Proverbs to "guard your heart" (4:23) with some emotional distance.

  — What risks come with a couple's establishment of emotional distance? What possible benefits?

  — When, if ever, has emotional distance been a conscious and talked-about choice in your marriage? In what ways was your relationship stronger afterward?

- **Physical Distance**—Sometimes, when all else fails, people must get away from each other until the hurt can stop. Distance can provide time to protect, time to think, time to heal, and time to learn new things.

  — When have you, or someone you know, needed to resort to physical distance to provide space for healing or safety to preserve partners and the marriage itself? Remember that physical distance can range from simply removing oneself from an argument to moving into a shelter with your children.

  — What risks come with a couple's establishment of physical distance? What possible benefits?

- **Other People**—God has always provided help from his spiritual family to those who need it.

  — What did you find encouraging about Sandy's experience? Identify both some risks and some benefits of turning to other people.

  — Who, if anyone, has helped you strengthen your boundaries? Whose care, support, teaching, and modeling might help you develop the spine you need to set and maintain healthy boundaries in your marriage? Or where could you go to find such people?

- *Time*—Time to work out a conflict or to limit the conflict is another boundary that structures difficulties in relationships.

  — When, if ever, have you used time as a boundary in your marriage?

  — Look again at the examples on page 34 of the text. What current issue in your marriage could benefit from one of these arrangements? Be specific about the issue and about the timing that might help you and your spouse deal with it.

Just as the physical world has different kinds of boundaries, the interpersonal world has different ones as well. Just as sometimes a fence is appropriate and a door is not, sometimes confrontation and truth are important and physical distance is not. Part III of this book offers guidelines to help you know when to do what.

Stephanie (page 34)

Stephanie was suffering from the emotional distance that being on the wrong end of a one-sided relationship creates. In some ways her story is more revealing of the need for good boundaries in a marriage. She was unhappy in the face of no overt problems. This can sometimes be the worst kind of misery.

- What lessons in instituting boundaries in marriage does Stephanie offer you?

• Explain why "boundaries are only built and established in the context of relationship. . . . The only place boundaries are real is within relationship."

• Why do clearly established boundaries lead to greater intimacy?

As Stephanie and Steve became more defined, they became two people who could love and be loved. They began to know and enjoy one another. They began to grow. And this is what we would like for you and your spouse. In this book we will help you become better defined, more free and responsible, and more in a position to love and be loved. This is the high calling God created marriage to be.

— *Lord,* —————————————————————

I'm seeing more clearly what a high calling marriage is! In order for me to respond to that calling, please help me learn to take ownership of my feelings, attitudes, and behaviors; to take responsibility for my choices, desires, thoughts, values, talents, and love; and both to grant my spouse freedom and to responsibly act on the freedom he or she grants me. Teach me to use boundaries for protection when appropriate and for self-control always. And give me wisdom as I use words, truth, consequences, emotional distance, physical distance, other people, or time to build or strengthen boundaries. And to you be the glory when our marriage is more like what you designed it to be! In Jesus' name. Amen.

Chapter 2

Applying the Ten Laws of Boundaries to Marriage

*B*oundary issues in marriage always require an understanding of the situation. Though we give practical suggestions throughout the book, in the long run, learning principles helps more than learning techniques. We have, therefore, included this section on the laws of boundaries, not as practical strategies, but as principles by which to structure your marriage. These laws of boundaries are not about marriage *as it should be. They are about marriage* as it really is. *Like the law of gravity, the laws of boundaries are always in force, whether or not we are aware of them. These laws lay the foundation of how responsibility works in life.*

Law #1: The Law of Sowing and Reaping (page 38)

Simply put, this principle means that our actions have consequences. When we do loving, responsible things, people draw close to us. When we are unloving or irresponsible, people withdraw from us.

- ***Playing and Not Paying***—Remember Randall and Amy? He was "playing," and she was "paying." And because of this, he was not changing his ways. Randall had no incentive to change, because Amy, not he, was dealing with his problem.

  — When in your marriage have you played but not paid—or where are you doing so now?

— When in your marriage has your spouse played but not paid—or where are you letting him or her do so now?

— In the first situation you just identified, what consequences should you have been experiencing? In the second, what consequences should you have allowed, or should you now allow, your spouse to experience?

- *Consequences Grow Spouses Up*—God designed marriage to be a place not only of love, but of growth. One pathway to growth is learning that actions have consequences.

  — When in your life—your married life or earlier—have consequences taught you a lesson and helped you grow up? Be specific.

  — Explain in your own words and, ideally, with an example from your life why boundaries are key to this Law of Sowing and Reaping. Also, why is allowing your spouse to reap the effects of selfishness or irresponsibility an act of love?

- **Relational and Functional Reaping**—The Law of Sowing and Reaping is played out in the two main areas of marriage: relationship and function.

  — The relational part of marriage involves the emotional tie two people have to each other, such as how deeply connected they are and how they feel about each other, both positively and negatively. In what way, if any, are you seeing the Law of Sowing and Reaping being played out or being short-circuited in the relational part of your marriage? Be specific.

  — The functional part of marriage has to do with the "doing" aspects of the relationship, such as paying bills, managing time, cooking meals, keeping house, and rearing children. In what way, if any, are you seeing the Law of Sowing and Reaping being played out or being short-circuited in the functional part of your marriage? Be specific.

  — What will you do to implement the Law of Sowing and Reaping in the situation(s) you just identified?

The Law of Sowing and Reaping is interrupted when the one who has the problem isn't facing the effects of the problem. And things don't change in a marriage until the spouse who is taking responsibility for a problem that is not hers decides to say or do something about it. Doing so helps place both the sowing and the reaping with the same person and begins to solve the boundary violation.

Law #2: The Law of Responsibility (page 41)

The Law of Responsibility is this: We are responsible to each other, but not for each other. Spouses may help each other with the loads of life (the financial, health, or emotional crises that come along), but ultimately, each person must take care of his own daily responsibilities (including one's feelings, attitudes, values, and handling of life's everyday difficulties).

- Review the discussion of the Law of Responsibility (pages 41–43). In what area of marriage, if any, are you neglecting your responsibility? Are you, for instance, failing to love your spouse? In what ways are you violating the Golden Rule and not treating your mate as you yourself would want to be treated?

- Also consider how you may be taking on responsibility that your husband or wife should be bearing. How, if at all, are you taking responsibility for your spouse's feelings, attitudes, values, or everyday difficulties? Or where are you allowing your spouse to take responsibility for your feelings, attitudes, values, or everyday difficulties?

- Finally, is one of you rescuing from or enabling the other to indulge in sinful or immature behavior? Describe the behavior as well as the rescuing or enabling.

- How can boundaries help in one or all of the situations you just identified? Be specific.

A proper view of responsibility is necessary to set limits in marriage. If one spouse feels no sense of responsibility to the other, this spouse is, in effect, trying to live married life as a single person. On the other hand, you can't cross the line of responsibility. You need to avoid taking ownership of your mate's life.

Law #3: The Law of Power (page 43)

The Law of Power clarifies what we do and don't have power over. We don't have the power to change others, but we can influence them. We do have the power to confess, submit, and repent of our own hurtful ways and then be willing to change.

- First, let's talk more about what we don't have power over. We have no power over the attitudes and actions of other people.

  — What about your spouse would you like to change? Reread the two preceding sentences. What is freeing about this fact?

  — What about yourself (your attitude, your response, etc.), in regards to what you just identified about your spouse, can you change—or, better, ask God to change?

  — What about yourself would you like to be able to change? Keep that in mind the next time you become frustrated with the behavior in your spouse that you would like to change. *You* don't have the power to be the person you would like to be, either.

• If you don't have the power to change your spouse, what *do* you have power over? As mentioned earlier, you do have the power to confess, submit, and repent of your own hurtful ways; to ask for God's help; to be willing to change; to identify ways you are contributing to your marriage problems; and, over time, to grow through the unhelpful ways you are dealing with those issues.

— Which one of these powers will you begin exercising this week?

— What specific step will you take?

• We don't have the power to change others, but we can influence them, and influence has its own power. What could you do to positively influence your spouse toward the change you would like him or her to make?

Spouses often try to use boundaries to assert power over a mate, and the tactic doesn't work. The fruit of the Spirit is self-control, not other-control (Galatians 5:23). Furthermore, nothing is more conducive to a spouse's growth than a mate who sincerely wants to change.

Law #4: The Law of Respect (page 45)

The Law of Respect states that if we wish for others to respect our boundaries, we need to respect theirs. We can't expect others to cherish our limits if we don't cherish theirs.

- We all get excited about finally being able to say no, set limits, and become free to choose, but we don't feel as excited about hearing no.

  — When did you last say no to your spouse? Describe the situation, focusing on how he or she reacted. On a scale of 1 to 10 (1 being Rodney Dangerfield: "I don't get no respect"), how respected did you feel? Why?

  — When did your spouse last say no to you? Again, describe the situation, focusing this time on how you reacted, internally as well as externally. On a scale of 1 to 10 (1 being Rodney Dangerfield), how respected did you feel? Why?

- The Law of Respect fosters love. Loving your mate means desiring and protecting her freedom of choice. It means dying to your wish for your mate to see things your way and appreciating that she has her own mind, values, and feelings.

  — Think again about the situation you just described. What did it show you about the relationship between respect and love?

  — Look at the bulleted questions on page 47. Make a date with your spouse to discuss these questions.

- If your spouse is untrustworthy, you can respect his boundaries and still set boundaries with his untrustworthiness.

  — Why do you describe your spouse as untrustworthy?

  — What limits can you set on the untrustworthiness you just described?

Respecting and valuing your mate's boundaries is the key to being close and loving. Your spouse experiences the gift of freedom from you and sees the love you are extending in giving this freedom. When you respect your spouse's boundaries, you are paving the way to having yours respected.

Law #5: The Law of Motivation (page 48)

The Law of Motivation states that we must be free to say no before we can wholeheartedly say yes. No one can actually love another if he feels he doesn't have a choice not to. Giving your time, love, or vulnerability to your spouse requires that you make your own choice based on your values, not out of fear.

- *Having* to do anything is a sign that someone is afraid.

  — Review the list of fears on page 49. Which of these, if any, has interfered with your efforts to set or maintain boundaries in marriage?

  — What step(s) might you take to mature through those fears—or who might be able to help you plan a course of action?

- Learning to pay attention to your motives does not mean saying yes only when you feel like it or want to do something. This is selfishness.

  — When have you made the uncomfortable and painful choice to sacrifice for your mate?

  — What motivated that choice?

To the extent that you are free to say no, you are free to say yes. This is why sometimes it is good to say, "I can't wholeheartedly say yes to this, so I'll have to say no at this time." After all, no spouse in his right mind really wants a mate who complies with his wishes out of fear.

Law #6: The Law of Evaluation (page 51)

We need to evaluate the pain our boundaries cause others. Do they cause pain that leads to injury? Or do they cause pain that leads to growth?

- Remember Trent and Megan?

  — What is the difference between pain and injury?

  — Before Trent set boundaries, what was being injured and who was feeling no pain?

— After Trent set boundaries, who felt pain? But what injury stopped happening—and what growth did Megan start to experience?

— What situation in your marriage, if any, does this story call to mind? Where might you or your spouse be incorrect in your evaluation of the other's pain?

- It is unloving to set limits with a spouse in order to harm him. But it can be just as unloving to avoid setting a limit with your spouse simply because you don't want him to be uncomfortable.

  — Are you currently being unloving in either of these ways? What will you do to rectify the situation?

  — In what aspect of your marriage would your spouse's establishment of boundaries be wise, but you realize that he or she is failing to set boundaries out of the fear of hurting you or making you uncomfortable? What will you do or say to help ease your spouse's fear?

  — When has pain been a good friend to you? You might share that story with your spouse as you, in response to the preceding question, encourage him to set limits with you.

Just because someone is in pain doesn't necessarily mean something bad is happening. Sometimes discomfort is an opportunity for growth. Do not neglect setting limits in your marriage because of a fear of causing pain. Pain can be the best friend your relationship ever had.

Law #7: The Law of Proactivity (page 52)

The Law of Proactivity is taking action to solve problems based on our values, wants, and needs. Proactive people solve problems without having to blow up.

- Review the discussion of the three facets of the Law of Proactivity (pages 53–54).

   — Where do you see yourself? Have you experienced your first tantrum? Do you have a season of reactive boundaries ahead of you? Or are you stuck in protest, defined more by what you hate than by what you love? Or are you disagreeing and confronting issues in your marriage without getting caught up in an emotional storm?

   — Where might your spouse be? Has he or she experienced that first tantrum? Does he or she have a season of reactive boundaries ahead? Or is your mate stuck in protest, defined more by what is hated than by what is loved? Or is your mate disagreeing and confronting issues in your marriage without getting caught up in an emotional storm?

   — What do your answers about yourself and your spouse tell you about your marriage?

- Look again at Eric and Jen, specifically the words Jen would have been wise to speak years ago (the end of the second paragraph on page 53). Based on this model, what can you say to be proactive regarding a current issue in your marriage?

Work on setting proactive boundaries in your marriage, deliberate boundaries built on love and based on your values.

Law #8: The Law of Envy (page 54)

The most powerful obstacle to setting boundaries in marriage is envy. The Law of Envy states that we will never get what we want if we focus outside of our boundaries on what others have. Envy is devaluing what we have, thinking it is not enough.

- The envious person doesn't set limits because he is not looking at himself long enough to figure out what choices he has. Instead, his envious eye is keeping himself focused on the happiness of others and how unfair that seems.

  — On a scale of 1 to 10 with 1 being bright white and 10 being dark, forest green, how envious are you?

  — And how envious is your spouse?

  — When, if at all, has the presence of envy in your marriage caused problems?

- Remember Bev and Jim?

  — What was Bev envying? And what problem was that envy causing in her marriage, specifically in her boundary setting?

  — What, if anything, does Bev and Jim's relationship help you see about your marriage?

You can't set limits in marriage until you are looking at yourself as part of the problem and as a great deal of the solution. Work through envy, own your problems, and take action.

Law #9: The Law of Activity (page 55)

The Law of Activity states that we need to take the initiative to solve our problems rather than being passive.

- Consider your marriage.

  — Is one of you the "active" spouse and the other the "passive" one? Identify who's who and explain why the labels fit.

  — If you consider yourself the "active" spouse, give two or three brief examples of your ability or tendency to take initiative. Also, share a mistake or two you have made and what you have learned from them.

— If you are the "passive" spouse, look at the reasons for passivity identified at the bottom of page 55 and the top of page 56. Why are you passive?

— If one spouse is active and the other passive, several problems can arise. Which ones listed on page 56 have you and your spouse encountered?

• All things being equal, active spouses have an edge in boundary setting.

— Why would being active, as opposed to being passive, facilitate boundary setting?

— What is appealing about the description of the two active spouses (page 56)?

— In what area of your marriage could you—and will you—take the initiative rather than merely wait for your spouse to act?

To clarify, the Law of Proactivity has to do with taking action based on deliberate, thought-out values rather than reacting emotionally. The Law of Activity has to do with taking the initiative versus being passive and waiting for someone else to make the first move.

Law #10: The Law of Exposure (page 57)

The Law of Exposure states that we need to communicate our boundaries to each other. When boundaries are "exposed," two souls can be connected in the marriage. But when boundaries are unexposed, spouses are less emotionally present in the marriage, and love struggles.

- Look again at the husband's behavior and then, on page 58, his hypothetical words.

    — What was his part in the dance? His wife's?

    — What does his wife lose when he doesn't reveal his boundaries?

    — What boundaries is he exposing?

- How can boundaries promote love and truth? (This was God's design.)

When we expose our boundaries to the light of relationship, we can be fully connected to our spouses. Exposure is the only way for healing and growth to take place.

Apply these laws to your marriage and see how they change the way you relate to each other. Remember, you can't break laws forever without consequences. Besides, these laws will help your marriage adapt to God's principles of relationship.

Again, Lord,

I find myself in awe of your design for marriage, and—as I read through these laws of boundaries in marriage—humbled by how far short of your standards I fall. I ask you to open my eyes to where the problems lie; to give me a heart that will love my spouse despite those problems; and to grant me the courage and wisdom to learn to act according to these laws of boundaries so that my marriage will indeed be informed by your principles. I pray in Jesus' name. Amen.

Chapter 3

Setting Boundaries with Yourself

Becoming More Lovable

Lynn was weary of Tom's chronic lateness in coming home from work. Reminding, nagging, and cajoling Tom had been ineffective. She put a two-point plan to work: she changed both her attitude and her actions. Finally, Tom structured the end of his day to get home on time, and Lynn's important family time became a reality. Why had Tom changed? "First, you were a lot nicer to me," he told Lynn. "I felt more like coming home. And second, I just hate reheating dinner."

Whose Problem Is It, Anyway? (page 61)

Lynn solved a small but chronic marriage problem by making an important shift in her attitude. She stopped trying to change Tom, and she started making changes in herself.

- Lynn moved from seeing the problem as Tom's lateness to seeing it as her unhappiness with Tom's lateness. Describe an ongoing problem in your relationship in terms that show it to be your problem, not your spouse's.

- First, Lynn reined in her impulse to attack Tom for his tardiness. She set a boundary on her anger. Second, Lynn set a limit on her enabling of Tom. She realized that she was making it easier for him to be irresponsible.

  — Consider the problem you described. What does Lynn and Tom's example suggest to you about an attitude of yours that you could change?

  — What does Lynn and Tom's example suggest about an action you could take to stop enabling your spouse?

When you cease to blame your spouse and own the problem as yours, you are then empowered to make changes to solve your problem.

The Chapter No One Wants to Read (page 62)

No one wants to read this chapter. We all want to find ways to say no to our spouse rather than to ourselves. Yet the ideas in this chapter may be the only hope for your marriage to develop a healthy set of boundaries.

- More often than not, the first boundaries we set in marriage are with ourselves. We deny ourselves certain freedoms to say or do whatever we'd like in order to achieve a higher purpose.

  — What boundaries with yourself have you set, however aware or unaware, to help make your marriage work?

  — What boundaries do you think your spouse has set for himself or herself to help make your marriage work?

- The reality of boundaries in marriage is that no matter what the issue in your marriage, you need to take the initiative to solve it. Though you may share no blame in creating the problem, you probably need to take some initiative in solving it.

  — When, if ever, have you failed to take initiative to solve a problem you didn't cause? Be specific about why you didn't and the results of your lack of effort.

  — Why is such a demand for "fairness" irrelevant?

God says that no matter who causes a problem, we are to take steps to solve it (Matthew 5:23–24; 18:15). God works this way also. He saw our lost state and took the first step of sending his Son to die to resolve a problem that was never his.

Removing the Plank (page 63)

Another reason we need to look first at our own boundaries on ourselves is that often we aren't blameless. Remember Scott and Molly's dance?

- Consider again the problem you've been thinking about in this chapter of the workbook. Scott sabotaged any real attempts to help Molly learn from the consequences of her financial irresponsibility. In what way(s) are you contributing to the problem in your marriage?

• Scott needed Molly to stay irresponsible so that he could continue his protest against all those irresponsible people in life. What might you lose if your spouse changed his or her problem behavior?

The "innocent" spouse needs to see what part, active or passive, he plays in the problem. Jesus called this the plank in our eyes (Matthew 7:5). This plank may be some attitude or emotion we aren't aware of that encourages the problem to continue.

Taking Ownership of Our Lives (page 64)

An important aspect of setting boundaries with ourselves is that of taking ownership of our lives. We need to take responsibility for our hearts, our loves, our time, and our talents. We are to own our lives and live in God's light, growing up and maturing our character along the way (Ephesians 4:15).

• Taking ownership of our lives is not as easy as it sounds. Blaming and setting boundaries with those we think sorely need limits comes much more easily.

— What are you blaming your spouse for? Your answer may indicate areas where you need to take ownership.

— What boundaries are you trying to set with your spouse? Again, your answer may indicate something about where you need to focus on yourself instead of your mate.

- Your spouse may be angry, irresponsible, inattentive, or self-centered. But you will not grow if you continue to react to these sins. This is not seeking first God's kingdom and righteousness (Matthew 6:33); it is seeking satisfaction from another person.

    — What sins or irritations are you reacting to in your marriage? Why do such reactions stunt your growth in Christlikeness?

    — We must become more deeply concerned about our own issues than our spouse's, for one day God will call us to account for our lives here on earth (2 Corinthians 5:10). If that moment of judgment came today, what would you say in your one-on-one conversation with God? Remember that you won't be able to blame, hide behind, or deflect to the sins and problems of your spouse.

Boundaries with yourself are a much bigger issue than boundaries in your marriage. You are responsible for half of your marriage and all of your soul. Boundaries with yourself are between you and God.

Being the "Good" Spouse (page 66)

In many marriages, one mate is more obviously selfish, irresponsible, withdrawn, or controlling. The other is perceived as a suffering saint. This often makes it hard for the "good" spouse to set appropriate boundaries for himself.

- In your relationship, are you the "good" spouse? If so, what is the "bad" spouse guilty of?

- If you or someone you know is the "good" spouse, which of the three reasons (listed below) makes setting boundaries difficult for you or that person? What might you do to get out of this trap of being "good"?

You are focusing more on your spouse's problems than your own
You feel helpless in the relationship because you don't have access to such helpful tools as truthfulness, honesty, limits, and consequences
You have taken a morally superior and dangerous position (Romans 3:10–18; 1 Corinthians 10:12).

Any time we focus on our goodness, we turn our hearts away from our need for love and forgiveness.

Living by the Same Rules (page 67)

We need to realize our need for limits because we need to submit ourselves to the same rules we want our partner to submit to.

- Submitting to the boundary process is the great equalizer in marriage and keeps both spouses in a mutual relationship instead of a one-up or one-down one. When it comes to boundaries, is your marriage a mutual relationship or a one-up or one-down one? Give specific details to support your answer.

- What brought the two of you to the situation you just described? Did a scene like the one described on page 67 (the husband would withdraw when the wife was not hearing him) help you both realize the need for boundaries—or is one of you not setting boundaries, resulting in a one-up or one-down relationship? And what keeps you in that dynamic of one-up and one-down?

Both spouses need to accept and respect the limits of the other; no one plays God, doing what he wants and expecting the other to comply.

Freeing Your Spouse by Setting Limits with Yourself (page 67)

When you set limits on yourself, you create an environment in which your spouse can become free to choose and grow.

- What changes in Andie enabled Brian to make important changes in himself?

- What does Andie and Brian's situation show you about your marriage? More specifically, what limits with yourself might free your spouse to change?

You cannot make your spouse grow up—that is between him and God. But you can make it easier for him to experience the love and limits he needs. When he faces the consequences of his immaturity, he stands a better chance of changing than if he faces your nagging and hounding. Become truthful, not controlling.

In the rest of the chapter, we will deal with the two major areas in which we need to set boundaries with ourselves in marriage. The first is our own character issues. The second is how we relate to our spouse's issues.

Setting Boundaries with Our Own Character (page 69)

The highest calling of a spouse is the call to love, just as it is the highest calling of our faith—loving God and each other (Matthew 22:37–40). Love means doing what you can for your spouse.

- What did you appreciate about Liz's approach to her less-than-satisfying marriage with Greg? When will you follow her lead and ask your spouse, "What do you see me doing that hurts or bothers you?"

- When, if ever, have you or your spouse set personal boundaries that made you or him better to live with? What current need is there for you to set boundaries on your own character?

Setting boundaries on your own character weaknesses is one of the most loving things you can do in your marriage. The spouse of someone who is growing spiritually should be better off, not worse off!

Process, Not Perfection (page 70)

When we look at our own character issues, we cannot will ourselves to maturity.

- We don't have the power to change our destructive behaviors and attitudes by just saying no (Romans 7:15).

  — What ongoing destructive behavior or attitude regularly reminds you of your inability to do what you want to do and not do what you don't want to do?

— Although we can't change our destructive behaviors and attitudes automatically, we do have some power and choices. Which of the following powers do you need to exercise, and when will you do so?

Choose to tell the truth about your faults
Choose to bring those faults into the light of relationship
Choose to repent of those faults and to work them out and mature from them

Again, although we can't change our destructive behaviors and attitudes automatically, we do have some power and choices. Here are some character issues on which we can set limits.

- **Playing God**—By human nature, we try to play God instead of seeking him. In doing so, we miss the mark in loving, being responsible, and caring about the welfare of our spouse.

  — In what specific ways, if any, are you trying to play God in your marriage relationship?

  — What steps will you take to submit this part of yourself to God's authority? See the top of page 71 for some suggestions.

- **Denial**—When we do not admit the truth about who we are, we give our spouse no one with whom to connect (1 John 1:8). What we deny about ourselves is absent from love.

  — What aspect of yourself, if any, are you denying? What failure, weakness, selfishness, or hurtfulness are you denying and rationalizing?

  — Ask God to prepare you and enable you to confess this tendency to your spouse—who most likely knows the truth anyway. At the same time, ask God to prepare your spouse to respond with compassion, support, and love. When will you confess what you have been denying? Be specific: set a time.

- **Withdrawal from Relationship**—Failing to make and keep emotional connections is a serious character issue. Such emotional isolation withdraws the most basic part of ourselves from the source of life: God. It damages our relatedness to God and others.

  — If you tend to withdraw, what do you think is behind that tendency? Do you struggle to trust? Do you fear that the relationship will control or hurt you? Does withdrawal help you feel safer and more protected?

  — Which of the three steps listed on pages 72 and 73 will you take to help set boundaries on this tendency to withdraw from relationship?

— If your spouse tends to withdraw, what might you do to help him first recognize, and then set boundaries, on that tendency?

- ***Irresponsibility***—Ever since the Fall, we have protested the reality that our lives are our problem and no one else's.

  — All of us desire either to have someone else take responsibility for us or to avoid the consequences of our actions. What evidence of this desire do you see in your own life? Do you, for instance, leave certain tasks undone at work or in your marriage? Do you argue when others say no? Be specific.

  — If you don't think you have a problem here, when will you ask your spouse in the off chance that you may?

  — If you have problems with responsibility, which of the three steps outlined on pages 73 and 74 will you take to help set limits on this behavior?

- ***Self-Centeredness***—Nothing is more natural than to think more of our own situation than another's. Thinking that the sun rises and sets only on us is one of the most destructive marriage-busting character issues. Marriage cannot be successfully navigated without our giving more of ourselves than we are comfortable giving.

— In what ways, if any, are you trying to live as a single person in your marriage? What unrealistic and self-centered dreams, if any (like wanting life to be put on hold the minute you return home from work), are interfering with your marriage?

— If you have problems with self-centeredness, which of the three steps outlined on pages 74 and 75 will you take to help set limits on this behavior?

• **Judgmentalism**—Many spouses struggle with judging, criticizing, and condemning others. They have difficulty accepting differences in others and see the differences as black and white.

— Love cannot grow in a climate of fear (1 John 4:18). Are you the "judge" in your marriage? When do you find yourself hating both the sin and sinner?

— If you have the "judge" role in your marriage, which of the three tasks outlined on page 75 will you undertake to help set limits on this behavior?

- Setting limits on ourselves sometimes simply involves taking over a troublesome emotion, behavior, or attitude within a supportive relationship instead of acting on it. What supportive relationship can you turn to—or where could you go to begin developing that kind of relationship?

The character issues outlined above can be major sources of distance and disharmony in marriage. Yet, when you own them, set limits on their hurtfulness, and submit them to God's process of growth, love can flourish.

Boundaries on Our Attempts to Control (page 76)

Of all the aspects of ourselves we need to set limits on, our tendency to control our spouse is probably the most crucial.

- When, if ever, have you felt controlled and noticed a sense of freedom disappearing and love's existence threatened?

- If there is any surefire way to destroy trust and love, control is it. We must give our love freely.

  — In what ways—implicit or explicit—are you saying to your spouse, "I will love you if you do this or that"?

— For help in answering the previous question, look again at the four indicators of controlling others listed on pages 76 and 77. Where do you see yourself in this list?

— You could also ask your spouse how he or she feels controlled by you.

God himself places such a high premium on our freedom that he shies away from forcing us to do things that would benefit us. He understands that we will never learn to love or respond to him without that costly freedom. We do well to follow his example.

In this next section we will shed light on the ways we attempt to control our partners, and we will also provide ways to set boundaries on this unfortunate tendency.

Control Comes in Different Flavors (page 77)

Remember Connor and Stacy, the opera and the baseball game? Both Connor and Stacy tried to take freedom from each other, which is the essence of control.

- Connor's blowup was an aggressive way to intimidate Stacy into changing her mind and a way to punish her for not keeping the score even between them. Stacy's breakdown was a more indirect way to punish Connor for his anger and also a means of getting him to change his mind. Neither one valued the free choices of his or her spouse.

  — Where, if at all, do you see yourself or your behaviors in Connor? In Stacy?

— How do you tend to respond to your spouse's free choices? Give an example or two. How would you like to be able to respond?

Let us look at some of the ways that, like Connor and Stacy, couples attempt to control each other.

• **Guilt**—Guilt messages are intended to make our spouse feel responsible for our welfare. Guilt controls by creating the impression that our spouse's freedom injures us. When our spouse chooses differently from us, we label him or her "unloving."

— When, if at all, was the most recent time you communicated the guilt message? What method, such as a wounded silence or an "If you really loved me . . ." or "How could you be so selfish . . ." statement, did you use? What would have been a healthier way to communicate your thoughts and feelings?

— When, if at all, was the most recent time your spouse communicated a guilt message? What means did he or she use? How did you respond—and how would you have liked to respond?

• **Anger**—Often, when one spouse wants something the other doesn't, the disappointed mate will become angry. Anger is our basic protest against the fact that we are not God and that we cannot control reality.

— Is anger a tool you use to attempt to control your spouse? If so, are you direct, throwing tantrums like Connor, or covert, being passive-aggressive or sarcastic? What threat(s) do you make? Why do you think you choose this behavior? What would be healthier?

— Does your spouse tend to use anger in an attempt to control you? If so, is he or she direct, throwing tantrums, or covert, being passive-aggressive or sarcastic? What threat(s) does he or she make? How do you respond—and how would you like to respond—to this anger?

- **Persistent Assaults on the Spouse's Boundary**—One person will say no, then the spouse will make attempt after attempt to change the other's mind by arguing, wheedling, and pleading until the other is worn down.

  — Do you tend to be like a strong-willed door-to-door salesperson when your spouse says no to you? What boundaries are you most unwilling to accept? Give an example. Why won't you respect his or her no and live with the boundary being set?

  — Does your spouse tend to be like a strong-willed door-to-door salesperson when you say no? What boundaries does he or she seem most unwilling to accept? Give an example. What might be a healthy way of dealing with your spouse's arguing, wheedling, and pleading?

- **Withholding Love**—Of all the ways we attempt to control, withholding love may be the most powerful. When one spouse disagrees, the other disconnects emotionally until the spouse changes to suit her.

    — Are you sometimes guilty as charged? When did you last resort to this means of control? What might have been a healthier way to deal with the situation?

    — Does your spouse ever withhold love in an attempt to control you? What might you do to make this attempt to control you ineffective?

Control does indeed come in different flavors, and none of them are healthy or helpful to the relationship.

Submitting to Boundaries on Our Control (page 79)

The spouse who truly loves his mate and wants her to grow spiritually will, at some point, desire to give up these attempts to control. He will be willing to relinquish these strategies in favor of granting freedom and love. Here are some of the ways you can set limits on your attempts at control.

- **Realize the Cost of Other-Control**—The cost of other-control is that you might get external compliance, but lose your spouse's heart.

    — What do you do that negates freedom and love? Look again at the types of control we reviewed in the previous section.

— What indication, if any, do you have that your behavior is sowing seeds of resentment or causing your spouse to be emotionally absent?

— If your spouse's attempts to control you are sowing seeds of resentment or causing you to be emotionally absent, what might you do to try to keep this dance from doing any more damage to your relationship? More specifically, what and how will you share with your spouse how you are responding to his or her attempts to control you?

• ***Ask Your Spouse to Let You Know How Your Control Affects Him***— Often, when the controlled spouse lets the controlling spouse know how hurtful and distant the attempts make him feel, the controlling spouse feels compassion for the pain and is better able to set limits on the control.

— When will you ask your spouse how your control—or your attempts to control him—affects him? How do you want to respond to the answer, both immediately and in terms of the action you will take?

— If and when your spouse were to ask you this question, how would you like to respond? What requests for alternative behavior would you suggest to your spouse?

- ***Experience Your Own Helplessness to Change Your Spouse***—You may need to realize that you live with someone whom you can't "make" do the right thing.

  — Why is control over your spouse so important to you?

  — Why is the realization that you can't change your spouse important to your attempts to stop trying to control him or her?

- ***Learn to Grieve***—Grief helps us to accept the truth and let go of things we can't change or have. When you allow your spouse freedom, you will often feel loss and sadness about losing what you desired from him.

  — In what ways will you allow yourself to experience grief? With whom, for instance, will you share your struggle to stop trying to control your mate?

  — What will you do to try to find new ways to adapt to your marriage? (Reading this book counts as one way!)

- **Work Through Dependency Issues**—If your spouse is the only person through whom you can get needs met, you will have a bent toward controlling him.

  — What sources of love, approval, truth, or forgiveness—other than your spouse—do you have in your life?

  — If your list of sources is short or nonexistent, where might you go to develop relationships that might one day offer you love, approval, or truth?

- **Be a Separate Person from Your Spouse**—Sometimes one mate will define herself by her mate and not by her own individual soul. Then, when her spouse disagrees or makes a different decision, she personalizes the difference as an attack against her.

  — What scene from your marriage, if any, came to mind as you read this section (pages 80–81)? Be specific about what happened. Were you or your spouse unable to be separate from the other's feelings?

  — Step back from the scene you just described. In the calmness that comes with distance from a situation, explain why the decision was not a personal action directed against the spouse, despite the spouse's (or your own) feelings.

- ***Value Your Spouse's Freedom As You Want Your Freedom Valued***—
  Jesus' Golden Rule of doing to others as you would have them do to you
  (Matthew 7:12) is the basis for how spouses are to treat each other.

  — How would you like your spouse to respond to your freedom? And what
  additional freedom would you like to experience in your marriage?

  — How would you like to be able to respond to your spouse's freedom?
  What additional freedom could you grant your spouse? In both cases,
  what barriers stand in the way of both your healthier response and
  greater freedom for your spouse—and what will you do to remove
  those barriers?

- ***Set Boundaries with Your Spouse Instead of Controlling Him***—
  Often a wife will resort to control strategies because she feels unable to
  say no or be free with her husband. Control becomes a substitute for establishing boundaries of self-control with her spouse. As you set appropriate limits, you can feel safe and give up controlling your partner.

  — What factors, such as the sense that you can't say no to your spouse,
  lie behind your control strategies?

  — What boundaries might you set for yourself so that you can feel safe
  and give up controlling your partner? The answer to this question
  may become clearer as you continue through *Boundaries in
  Marriage*.

As you can see, marriage has more to do with bringing yourself under the control of God and his principles than it does with controlling your spouse. However, as you relinquish control of your partner, you are able to better love him, protect your own freedom, and provide a context for both of you to grow.

In the next chapter we will show you how important it is for you to be a separate person from your spouse. Ironically, being an individual is the key to becoming one with your mate.

Dear God,

Again, Lord God, I am humbled by how much growing I have ahead of me as well as by the fact that boundaries are basically an issue between you and me. In light of that fact, I pray that you will show me where I need to take responsibility and set boundaries with myself; where I need to take ownership of my heart, my love, my time, and my talent; where I need to stop blaming; and where I need to be sure I'm living by the same rules I want my spouse to live by. Help me to set boundaries with myself and to have the courage, energy, and insight to do the work on the character issues that are weak. I submit to you this process of growth. I ask you not only to guide me but also to bless my efforts. Make me more like Christ, more loving *and* more lovable, a person who lives the Golden Rule he taught. In his name I pray. Amen.

Part Two

Building Boundaries in Marriage

Chapter 4

It Takes Two to Make One

*O*neness. *It's what the word* romance *is made of—and it's God's very design for marriage (Genesis 2:18; Mark 10:7–8). But oneness is more than that first stage of falling in love when a couple give up all internal boundaries and feel a euphoric sense of merging with each other. These experiences are not real oneness. They are only a preview. Real oneness is built over time as a relationship grows and as "two become one."*

In this chapter we will examine how every married couple needs to grow. We will look first at the prerequisite of "two becoming one." The prerequisite is that, for two to become one, we must have two *at the outset. Two complete individuals. What does this mean? And what does this have to do with boundaries?*

"Twoness" (page 86)

The requirement for oneness is two complete people.

- The Bible defines a complete person as a mature person. A complete person is able to do all the things that adult life and relationship require: give love and receive love, be independent and self-sufficient, live out values honestly, be responsible, have self-confidence, deal with problems and failures, live out one's talents, and have a life.

  — No one has ever made it to adulthood perfectly ready for all that it requires. Which of the qualities listed above did you not bring to your marriage?

— What problems have arisen in your marriage at least in part because you were less than complete in these ways?

- Marriage is not meant to be the place where one gets completed as a person. It is meant for complete persons to come together and build a "we" that is bigger and better than either one of the "I's" involved.

    — In what ways, if at all, did you hope—consciously or subconsciously— to be completed by marriage? What personal weaknesses did you expect your spouse to pick up the slack for?

    — On a more positive note, what glimpses, if any, have you had in your marriage of the "we" being bigger and better than either "I" involved? Or, to paraphrase Frederick Buechner (page 87), when have you sensed yourself becoming "more richly" yourself as a result of being married than you ever could have become on your own? Be specific.

Marriage is an adult contract, and you should not attempt it without two adults present! For a marriage to work, two separate individuals need to have some elements of adulthood. Again, no one has ever made it to adulthood ready for all that it requires. But you can grow toward this adulthood, and as you do, your relationship will attain more and more oneness as well. But before we take a look at the requirements of adulthood, we would like to make one more important point about two becoming one.

Completing Versus Complementing Each Other (page 87)

As we said above, marriage was not designed to complete a person. It was designed for two complete people to enter into and form something different than either of them is on his or her own.

- Many people see marriage as a shortcut to completeness or maturity. In what ways, if any, did you marry out of weakness, rather than strength? What did your spouse offer you that made up for what you did not possess on your own?

- The crucial element of "two becoming one" is that the two people must be complete in and of themselves—they must be adults—before they marry. Think about yourself and your spouse. What characteristics allow you to *complement* each other, not *complete* each other? More specifically, what different perspectives, talents, abilities, experiences, and other gifts does each of you bring to the relationship to form a partnership? List them below.

  My Mate   **Me**

  _____   _____

  _____   _____

  _____   _____

  _____   _____

  _____   _____

Completing means making up for one's immaturity as a person. It is an attempt to use another person to balance an imbalance in one's character, and it never works. Each person is responsible for working on these character imbalances on one's own and then bringing a whole, balanced self into the relationship.

- ***Areas of Completeness That Marriage Cannot Provide***—Many times people will marry to make up for what they do not possess in their own character.

    — Remember Amanda and Eric? What ingredients missing in their own personality did they find in each other? And, on a more positive note, what talents and skills made Amanda and Eric good complements to each other?

    — Basic human requirements of character are not complements. They are essentials that both partners must possess and that cannot be "borrowed" from each other. Review the list of abilities (pages 91–92). Which of these do you need to work on developing for yourself? Which do you need to learn to express?

Having identified some of the characteristics you need to develop, consider now how you can become a complete, mature, and whole person. Let's look at exactly what the requirements of adulthood are.

Adults Take Responsibility for Their Treasures (page 92)

The first requirement of adults, or completed persons, is that they take responsibility for all of the treasures of their souls (listed on page 92). If they don't, their marriage will stagnate to the degree that they disown aspects of their lives and then either blame the other or require the other to fix it or make up for it.

- Which treasures are you failing to take ownership of, perhaps instead relying on your partner to fix it or make up for it?

- Happiness is a treasure we need to take responsibility for, but for instance, a wife may not take responsibility for how she feels and blame her partner when she feels unhappy.

  — When, if at all, have you seen a husband or wife depend on the other for happiness? What were the results of that dependence?

  — In what ways, if any, are you depending on your partner for happiness and completeness?

Each person needs to take ownership of her own treasures, which we talked about in chapter 1. Second, each person needs to require her spouse to take ownership as well, which we will talk about now.

Requiring Ownership (page 93)

Codependency is taking responsibility for another person's problems and not requiring that person to take responsibility for his own. A mature, complete adult not only takes responsibility for himself, but also requires the same from the people he loves.

- To be codependent and not require responsibility from others is to not be responsible oneself. Consider again Maggie and Scooter.

  — Which of Maggie's demands would Scooter be wise to say no to?

— Which feelings and attitudes would Scooter's no force Maggie to take responsibility for?

— What, if anything, does looking at Maggie and Scooter's situation help you see about your relationship and either your or your mate's codependency?

- One of the greatest gifts we can give to each other is the gift of honesty and confrontation.

  — When have you received these important gifts from someone? (Ideally, choose a situation involving your spouse.) How did you benefit?

  — What, if anything, keeps you from giving the gifts of honesty and confrontation to your mate? What might you do to overcome these barriers?

We grow when someone who loves us "wounds" us by telling us painful truths we need to hear (Proverbs 27:6). Requiring responsibility from each other by telling each other the truth and not giving in to teach other's immaturity is indeed a gift.

Adults Value Their Treasures and Those of Their Spouse (page 95)

In the opening story of this book, Stephanie had ignored her own treasures and had not valued them in the marriage enough to ensure they were getting developed. She had ignored her feelings, her attitudes, and her talents while she was "living for Steve."

- We can't ignore aspects of our soul that God has placed in us. Sooner or later, brushing them aside catches up with us.

  — What treasures of your soul have you ignored, consciously or subconsciously? In what ways are they catching up to you?

  — What treasures do you think your spouse may be ignoring? In what ways are they catching up to your mate and to your marriage?

- Mature people think of nurturing, developing, and taking care of the treasures of the people with whom they are in relationship. They are always thinking of how their loved ones are doing, how they are feeling, and how they could help them grow.

  — When have you seen this kind of care in a marriage other than your own? What did you appreciate or respect in what you saw? How did this care strengthen the relationship?

— In what recent situation would you have done well to think more about how your spouse was doing or feeling or how you could help your spouse grow?

"Not wanting to miss out" is a good way to think of valuing the treasures of your spouse's soul. To value the treasures in the soul of your spouse is to not miss out on a wonderful gift from God to the both of you. This process of valuing others' treasures acknowledges the separateness and completeness of the other person. It says, "I know you are a person, too, and I am interested in the person you are."

Adults Understand the Concept of "You Are Not Me" (page 96)

The concept of "you are not me" is one of the most important aspects of boundaries. We are not extensions of each other. Instead, we are all individuals in our own right. We all need to overcome the basic egocentricity of life, the inborn feeling that "the world revolves around me." There are several components to this issue.

- *Seeing the Other as a Person, Not an Object*—The first component is the ability to see your spouse as a separate person, distinct from you, with her own needs and feelings. In other words, she doesn't exist just to meet your needs.

  — Remember Sally and Jim? When, if at all, have you been guilty of reducing others (perhaps your spouse) to objects of your own needs—or when have you been treated like that?

— Whether or not you have experienced it firsthand, describe what such treatment does to a relationship.

Whenever we view others only in terms of how they affect us, we are in big trouble. This is self-centeredness. Whenever we don't see people for who they really are, love breaks down.

- **Allowing the Other's Experience**—The second way in which we allow others to exist in their own right is to allow their experience. We need to put our own experience aside and join in the other's experience. The ability to do this is called *empathy*.

  — Why is empathy described as "the bedrock of intimacy"?

  — "If I can't allow you to be a person in your own right, I'll always take your experience as meaning something about me." When, if ever, have you seen this dynamic play itself out in your marriage? More specifically, when have you construed your mate's experience to mean something about you? When has your mate construed your attempt to express an experience to mean something about him or her?

To have good boundaries is to be separate enough from the other person that you can allow her to have her own experience without reacting with your own. Such a clear stance of separateness allows you not to react, but to care and empathize.

- ***Allowing the Freedom to Be Different***—The third way in which we allow others to exist in their own right is allowing them the freedom to be different from us. Whether or not a couple can get to oneness will depend on how okay it is to have two opinions, moods, tastes, or needs in the relationship at once.

  — What differences between you and your spouse came to mind as you read this section?

  — In what ways, if at all, do you and your spouse show that you value each other's differences? How do you show respect for those differences? Be specific. Or is one of you not allowed to be different from the other? Again, be specific about the issue(s) involved.

  — "The differences are what you like about a person at the beginning of a relationship and then fight about for the rest of your lives!" Which differences that initially attracted you to each other now drive one or both of you crazy? What does the fact of that initial attraction mean to you?

Differences are exciting and bring a sense of getting to enjoy something we don't possess. But differences threaten us if we have not matured enough to be truly separate people from each other. The ability to tolerate your spouse's differences is an important aspect of boundaries in marriage. When "twoness" exists, oneness can develop.

- ***Cherishing the Other's Existence***—Another part of the "you are not me" concept is the ability to see another person for who she is apart from what we want or need from her and to love and appreciate that person for who she is.

  — Remember Robert and Susan's dance class? Robert loved something about Susan that had nothing to do with him. She was just being herself, and he was gaining pleasure from just knowing her and experiencing her. He cherished her just as she was, for just who she was. When, if at all, have you chosen to love your spouse in that way? What aspects of your mate's existence could you choose to cherish (rather than, perhaps, complain about or ridicule) just as Robert cherished Susan's love for dance?

  — When, if at all, have you experienced this kind of love from your spouse? What does, or could, that kind of love do for your marriage?

  — What characteristics, interests, or talents of your mate give you, or could give you, the opportunity to express joy in just knowing him or her?

To cherish someone's existence apart from you and apart from what you get from that person requires very good boundaries, the ability to see the other person as distinct and separate from you. This aspect of love gives much pleasure as couples grow together.

Adults Respect Each Other's Freedom (page 101)

Freedom is a prerequisite of love. If someone controls us, love is not possible. Control results in slavery, not love. The ability of each partner to allow the other to be a free, separate person is one of the hallmarks of a solid relationship.

- *Free to Have Space*—Mary liked the connection with Rich, but she also allowed him to be his own person with his own time and space. And this was not just a sacrifice on her part. It was part of her completeness as a person. She had her own interests as well. This balance of being deeply connected *and* free to be individuals is one of the most important aspects of completeness.

  — In what ways are you and your spouse deeply connected? Be specific.

  — What freedom does each of you have to be an individual? What activities reveal your separateness from each other?

  — When, if ever, have you noticed that keeping your individuality and space actually strengthens your relationship?

  — But when, if ever, have you or your spouse seen time apart, separateness, and space as a threat, a lack of love, or abandonment?

- There is no certain amount of separateness that is good or bad for all couples. The amount has to be negotiated with wisdom so that the "we" does not suffer. But couples who have a fundamental orientation toward freedom are able to work out those details.

  — Freedom is the scariest of all human privileges. When have you seen (perhaps in your own marriage) freedom used by someone to indulge his or her own desires at the expense of the marriage?

  — When have you been guilty of getting selfish and falling back into the inborn egocentricity talked about earlier?

  — The Bible offers the best solution for the danger inherent in freedom: "Love your neighbor as yourself." Start doing so now by considering how your exercise of your freedom is affecting your spouse. Would you like to be treated the way you're treating your spouse? What changes in your behavior does this look in the mirror suggest?

  — Now, again applying the Golden Rule, are you trying to control your spouse's separateness and freedom with guilt and prohibition? Again, would you like to be treated that way? And what changes in your behavior does this look in the mirror suggest?

- **Good Fear of Reality**—If the Golden Rule doesn't stop you, maybe fear will.

  Controlling spouses often stop being that way when the fear of reality—the probable consequences—invades their hearts.

    — Step back from your marriage relationship. In your efforts to control your spouse, how (if at all) have you become like a parent or like the master of a slave?

    — What reality or consequence for being master or parent to your spouse did you read about in this section?

  Give freedom and require responsible use of that freedom in the service of love.

Longing (page 105)

God designed human beings with a longing for relationship, with a longing to come together and not go through life alone.

- Freedom nourishes separateness, which is in and of itself an undesirable state. Therefore, freedom from each other ironically creates the very longing that will bring you together over and over again. When has being separate from your spouse created a longing to be with him or her? Be specific about the value of that kind of experience.

• This paradox of separateness and togetherness is one of the balancing truths in God's universe. If you have too much separateness, you have no relationship because you become too disconnected. But if you have no separateness, you also have no relationship because there are no longer two people involved.

— In which direction do you tend to err in your marriage? What do you do to move the relationship in either unhealthy direction?

— What do you do, or could you do, to keep separateness and togetherness in healthy balance?

See the need for freedom as part of God's design, and find the right balance between togetherness and freedom for the two of you. Make sure you have both. If you give freedom, you will have longing. If you have togetherness, you will create more love that gives rise to more freedom to express who you are becoming. Nurture friends, hobbies, work, and time apart, and they will come back to you many times over.

Creator God,

Please work in me the maturity I need to bring to my marriage so that my spouse and I can know the oneness you intend for us. Show me areas I need to work on and guide that work. Teach me to complement my spouse, not try to complete him/her, and help me let my spouse complement me, not try to complete me. Give me energy and perseverance as I work to correct the imbalances in my character. Help me to value my spouse's treasures as well as my own; to develop heartfelt empathy for my mate; and to give him/her freedom, including the freedom to be different from me. And, finally, may I not depend on my spouse for happiness. May I focus instead on loving my mate, my closest neighbor, as myself. I pray in Jesus' name. Amen.

Chapter 5

What You Value Is What You'll Have

On both the positive and the negative side, ultimately what you value is what you will have. If you value something in a relationship, you will not tolerate anything that destroys this value, and you will also seek to make sure it is present and growing. What you value happens, and what you don't value will be absent.

- Your values make sure that certain bad things are not present in the marriage and that certain good things are. The values become the ultimate identity and protective boundaries of the marriage.

  — What bad things are not present in your marriage because of the values that you and your spouse hold?

  — What good things are present in your marriage, and what do you seek to have in your marriage because of the values that you and your spouse hold?

What you value determines the kind of relationship you most likely will have in the end. For this reason, we want to introduce six values that, if you hold them up high, esteem them, and pursue them as a couple, will help you build your relationship on solid ground and cause it to grow in the direction God intends.

The Worst Value Ever (page 108)

Before we look at the six important values we want you to lift up, let's first look at the worst value ever.

- Remember the client who wasn't ready for a relationship with anything— much less anyone—more demanding than a goldfish? People who always want happiness and pursue it above all else are some of the most miserable people in the world. When, if ever, have you pursued happiness for happiness' sake and found yourself miserable? Or when have you seen that in someone else?

The pursuit of happiness can result in misery because happiness is a result—usually the result of our being in a good place inside ourselves and our having done the character work we need to do so that we are content and joyful in whatever circumstances we find ourselves.

- Happiness is a fruit of a lot of hard work in relationships, career, spiritual growth, or a host of other arenas of life. But nowhere is this as true as in marriage.

  — What kind of hard work have you invested in a specific area of life and have found happiness as a result? Be specific about the area, the effort, and the resulting happiness.

  — When have you been happiest in your marriage? What kind of hard work contributed to that happiness?

- Marriage is a lot of work. Read again the second and third paragraphs on page 110 of the text.

  — Which of the difficult moments listed in the second paragraph have you recently encountered in your marriage? Give one or two examples.

  — Did you and your spouse choose to work through those difficult moments? If so, what did that work entail—and what resulted?

  — Or did you and your spouse try to ignore the difficulty or refuse to solve the problem? What course of action would you take if you could turn back the clock?

- If happiness is our guide and it goes away momentarily, we will assume that something is wrong. The truth is (and this is why happiness is such a horrible value), when we are not happy, something good may be happening.

  — Looking back now, describe a time when this statement was true for you, a time when you were not happy but something good was happening in you and therefore in your marriage.

— What current issue in your marriage may in fact be an opportunity for great growth? What will you do to embrace that issue?

- Before leaving this chapter, look again at the story of the driver who runs into trees (page 111). Now consider how you may be like that driver.

  — What "trees" are you running into?

  — What "car" are you thinking about selling so that you won't keep running into trees?

  — In actuality, what are you contributing to your pattern of hitting trees? What hard work is necessary for you to graduate from hitting trees and become a complete driver, in the terms of James 1:2–5?

- Many things are better to worry about than happiness, and these are the things that ultimately will produce happiness.

  — How high on your list of goals in life and in marriage is happiness?

— What would be some better things to worry about than happiness? (We've given you six possibilities on page 112!)

— Why might the pursuit of those things you just listed ultimately produce happiness?

Be willing to do the hard work of growth now, no matter how it feels, and happiness will likely find you. Don't have the worst value ever: "I must be happy at all times, and I value that more than anything else. Even more than growth." Happiness will certainly elude you.

The Big Picture (page 112)

There are two kinds of people in the world: those who focus on what they want, always desiring it and never attaining it, and those who focus on what it takes to obtain what they want. The latter do the work, delay gratification, make sacrifices, and ultimately get the rewards of their work.

- Into which category do you fall? Give an example or two from your life to support your answer.

- What does your previous answer suggest to you about what you are bringing to your marriage? Put differently, what can you do in your marriage to cultivate the garden instead of demanding the fruit? Be specific.

In the next six brief chapters we will take a closer look at why love of God, love of your spouse, honesty, faithfulness, compassion and forgiveness, and holiness can help you build a marriage that lasts. At this point, we want once more to encourage you to make cultivating these six values of prime concern. Work on them. Stand against anything in yourself or your spouse that would destroy them. And do everything you can to increase their presence. Pursue them with everything the two of you can muster—time, money, energy, focus—and they will not fail you in the end.

Lord God,

As I get ready to look at some of the fundamental values for married couples to hold, I ask that you would soften my heart toward my spouse and toward this process. Show me where I am running into trees—and what I'm contributing to that pattern. Make me willing to do the work that I will realize needs to be done, and give me energy for those efforts. Keep me seeking your values, not my happiness. And when I'm not happy, help me to trust that something good, some solid growth, is happening. Finally, help me stand against anything in myself or my spouse that would destroy love of God, love of my spouse, honesty, faithfulness, compassion and forgiveness, and holiness in my marriage and to do everything I can, by your grace, to increase their presence. I pray in Jesus' name. Amen.

Chapter 6

Value One

Love of God

---

*R*emember the couple who had given up hope in their relationship? I trusted their faith in God. "I know you both love God enough to make the changes that he wants you to make, and if you do that, I promise you that you will do very well in your relationship. Can you both commit to doing what God is going to ask of you in this process?"

• Jesus said that the greatest commandment is to love God with every ounce of yourself: "with all your heart and with all your soul and with all your mind and with all your strength" (Mark 12:30). One reason why he placed this value above all others relates to marriage. When loving God is our orienting principle, we are always adjusting to what he requires from us.

— When, if ever, have you obeyed God's call to change and have seen your marriage improve?

— In regard to what current issue in your marriage might God be calling you to change? Be specific about that change and about your hesitation to work that hard.

The call to change may strike us as unfair or too difficult or painful. But if we know that it's God with whom we ultimately have to deal, we submit to this reality and his higher calling to us to grow. In the end the relationship wins.

• Look again at the issues that the "hope-less" couple had to deal with (pages 114–115). Notice the attitudes and behaviors that God was calling on them to change.

  — Which of these items mentioned (judgmentalism, sarcasm, not wanting to listen, wanting to avoid conflict, bitterness and fears, blame) are issues for you to deal with in your marriage relationship?

  — Comment on the role that submission to God plays in building a stronger marriage. What behaviors, attitudes, habits, and so on is God calling you to submit to him so that, by the power of his Spirit, he can change you?

God's ways work. If you follow those ways—if you make a commitment to love God and follow through with the day-to-day work he asks you to do— your marriage will work. When God asks you to grow and change and you submit to him, your marriage will work.

• The "hope-less" couple loved God enough to do what he asked of them, and they grew to love each other as a result. The love that they now have for each other is a fruit of loving God.

  — Loving God must be first because he empowers us to change and tells us how to change. When have you known God's power to help you change? Be specific.

— Most of all, God becomes the one who keeps us from being ultimately in charge. If we try to be in charge, we will do it our way, and then our own limitations become the limitations of the relationship as well. In what aspects of your marriage are you trying to be in charge? How, if at all, are your ways in these areas contradictory to God's ways? And which of your limitations are limiting your marriage?

• Think back over the chapter. For what specific action, statement, effort, or attitude in regard to his or her love of God can you affirm your spouse? Do so!

Love God first, with all of your heart, mind, soul, and strength. Lose your life to him, and you will gain it.

Father God,

Help me to love you enough to make the changes that you want me to make and to stand strong in my commitment to do whatever you ask of me in this process of growing in character and strengthening my marriage. May your love truly be the orienting principle in all I do in and for my marriage. Help me to submit to you, All-loving, All-wise Father and Designer of marriage. Tell me how to change, and empower me to obey. In Jesus' name I pray. Amen.

Chapter 7

Value Two

Love of Spouse

The love that builds a marriage is the kind of love God has for us. It is called "agape." Agape is love that seeks the welfare of the other. It is love that has nothing to do with how someone is gratifying us at the moment. It has to do with what is good for the other. In short, agape is concerned with the good of the other person.

Jesus said it this way in the second greatest commandment: "Love your neighbor as yourself." When we do that, we are truly loving someone. Let's look at three things loving someone "as yourself" means in marriage.

• First, you so deeply identify with your spouse that you feel the effects of your own behavior on your spouse. In a counseling session, Scott looked past his behavior (angry outbursts, aggressive communication) to the effects of his behavior (Maria's fear). He saw what it was like to be on the other end of a relationship with him.

— To deeply identify with another person is to think about the effects of your behavior on that other person. It is to get out of the self-centeredness of just acting to please oneself. Think back over your interactions with your spouse this past week. When were you acting in word and deed solely to please yourself? Give two or three specific examples.

— How did your spouse react to those moments you just listed?

— What would it have been like to be on that end of a relationship with you?

How would you like to be treated? Would you like your spouse to do to you what you are doing to your spouse? This identifying with another's experience is called empathy. And empathy empowers you to seek the best for the other person because it puts you in touch with her life and how it feels to be her, especially on the other end of a relationship with you.

• Second, loving your spouse as yourself means you think of making your spouse's life better. What would you like if you were in your spouse's situation?

— What is your spouse's current situation? What stress is he or she under? What responsibilities, worries, or hurts is he or she carrying? What decisions, frustrations, or transitions is he or she facing?

— Now list what you would like if you were in your spouse's situation, the situation you just described. What will you do to give the items on your list to your spouse?

When you feel the other person's need as your own (empathy) and you sacrifice to meet it, you also find joy in the happiness and fulfillment that she finds.

- Third—and this is the most difficult to grasp—loving your spouse as yourself means you want the best for your spouse even when your spouse can't see what that is.

  — When, if ever, have you had the opportunity to love your spouse in this way? What did you do—or what do you wish you had done?

  — When, if ever, has your spouse had the opportunity to love you in this way? Describe the situation and the growth that occurred if your spouse acted courageously and loved boldly.

  — What current opportunity, if any, do you have to love your spouse in a way that your spouse may not initially experience as love? What does this discussion of love motivate you to do?

This kind of love may cost you. But it would be good. And to love her as yourself means that you want it for your spouse as desperately as you would want it for yourself.

Commitment (page 120)

In addition to being based in empathy, this kind of love is based in commitment. Again, this is best seen in the kind of love God has for us. God's word for this kind of commitment is covenant.

- To commit to someone means that you will be there and that you will stay, even when things get difficult.

  — When have you and your spouse stayed in the marriage—emotionally as well as physically—and worked through a difficult time? What kept you from leaving? Moreover, what rewards came from hanging in there and going through the necessary changes?

  — What current challenge is calling for you to stand on the commitment you made to your spouse?

  — Think back on the analogies of the marathon runner (when does she see the finish line?) and the patient in surgery (what happens if he decides to get off the table in the middle of the operation?). What encouragement do you find for the present, or for whatever challenge may lie ahead, in these two comparisons?

In marriage, commitment provides the time, structure, and security needed for growth and change to take place. Commitment keeps the patient on the table until the surgery is finished.

• Commitment also provides something else necessary for growth: security. Without the security that commitment provides, partners know at some deep level that if they do not perform up to some expectation, they could be forsaken. And performance anxiety always inhibits real change.

— When has performance anxiety been a factor in your marriage and kept you from pursuing personal growth? If that kind of anxiety is no longer an issue for you, to what do you attribute the change?

— Could performance anxiety be an issue for your spouse? What can and will you do to let your mate know that you are committed to him or her and that you aren't going to leave?

• Commitment drives the *need* for growth as well as the *security*. If you're going to be with someone for the long term, it's best to work things out. Commitment often drives one toward resolution.

— When has the fact that you're in your marriage for the long term compelled you to deal with an issue? Explain what happened and how your commitment to the marriage kept you working.

— What issue in your marriage, if any, that you've been ignoring, hoping it would go away, does this statement encourage you to address?

As one married man put it, "It is a totally different life when you know that the one who loves you is never going to go away. It changes you at a very deep level."

Action (page 121)

Without action, James says, faith is dead (James 2:17). There is no such thing as a faith that doesn't produce action. The same is true for love. Love is not just a feeling or an attachment to a person. Love is an expression of that attachment. The love that brings good boundaries to a marriage is the love that brings action to the relationship as well.

- The more familiar they are with someone, the lazier people get.

  — In the early days of your courtship and marriage, what actions did you take to express your love to your spouse?

  — In what ways have you gotten lazy? Which of the actions you just listed will you once again start doing—beginning this week?

- True love will not allow itself to go cold. When it does, there is a call to action, a call to rekindling the flame.

  — What sign(s) are you aware of that your love for your spouse needs some rekindling?

— Again, what steps will you take to rekindle your love, to not allow your love for your spouse to go cold?

As Jesus says of our relationship to God, "do the things you did at first" (Revelation 2:5). The need for action in a love relationship never goes away.

A Picture (page 122)

Love is the foundation for marriage: love for God and love for another person.

- Love expresses itself in seeking the best for the other person no matter whether he deserves it or not. It places the other person above one's own selfish needs and desires. It sacrifices, gives, and suffers. It weathers hurts and storms for the long-term preservation of the covenant.

  — Which aspect(s) of love listed here did you need to be reminded of right now? Why? Ask God to be with you as you live out love in your marriage as he intends you to.

  — What past experiences does this list affirm the value of? What growth has resulted because you and your spouse have done one or more of the above?

- Make love your highest value in your marriage. For in the end, love is the strongest power at your disposal.

  — If you make love the highest value in your marriage, it is likely to return the commitment you make to it. When have you seen your efforts to love your spouse rewarded? Be specific.

  — Read 1 Corinthians 13:4–8a again. What dimension(s) of love listed here need special attention in your marriage? Make that a topic of prayer, perhaps prayer of confession as well as supplication.

- Think back over chapter 7. For what specific action, statement, effort, or attitude in regard to loving can you affirm your spouse? Do so!

None of us is able to live out the 1 Corinthians description of love completely, but as we try, love will serve as a powerful boundary against all sorts of evil. It will protect your relationship and give you many, many returns for all that you invest in its enduring power.

Lord,

Agape love is a tall order! Help me, God, to deeply identify with my mate, to think about the effects of my behavior on him/her and to get out of the self-centeredness of just acting to please myself. Enable me to work on making my spouse's life better, to regularly ask myself, "What would I like if I were in my spouse's situation?" And, when appropriate, help me to love my spouse as myself by wanting the best for him/her even when he/she can't see what that is. Besides empathy, grant me the grace to be true to my covenant commitment to my mate. And show me—guide me—in the actions I need to take to strengthen our marriage. Fill me with your love so that I can place my mate above my own selfish needs and desires, so that I can sacrifice, give, and suffer, so that I can weather the hurts and storms that come with marriage. I pray in Jesus' name. Amen.

Chapter 8

Value Three

Honesty

I *just need to know the truth," Rachel explained. "I can deal with what-ever it is. If Richard would just tell me the truth, I could handle it. But I can't handle all the surprises. The lies are killing me."*

- Deception damages a relationship. The act of lying is much more damaging than the things that are being lied about, because lying undermines the knowing of one another and the connection itself. The point at which deception enters is the point at which relatedness ends.

  — When has someone (your spouse or otherwise) been less than honest with you? What impact did that deception have on your relationship with that person?

  — When have you been less than honest with someone? What impact did your deception have on your relationship with that person?

- Couples deceive each other in many ways. Sometimes spouses lie over small things. At other times, they lie about serious things.

  — Deception can happen through hypocritical behavior and feigned attitudes as well as false words. In what ways, if any, have you been deceiving your spouse? Be specific.

  — What path of repentance and confession will you take? Who might you choose to pray for you and hold you accountable to regaining integrity in all that you do and all that you say?

In our way of thinking, anything, large or small, is forgivable and able to be worked through in a relationship—except deception. Deception is the one thing that cannot be worked through because it denies the problem. It is the one unforgivable sin of a relationship because it makes forgiveness unattainable.

Some Guidelines (page 125)

We believe in total honesty. But, honesty must go along with the other values we have discussed. Honesty without love and commitment can wreck a tenuous connection. Honesty without forgiveness can do the same. Honesty without a commitment to holiness does not give the offended spouse a reason for hope that the problem will not reoccur.

- Which of the following areas do you find difficult to be honest about with your spouse?

  Feelings
  Disappointments
  Desires, likes, and dislikes
  Hurts
  Anger and hatred
  Sex
  Sins
  Failure
  Needs and vulnerabilities

- Now consider carefully the areas you selected.

  — Why are the items you chose especially difficult for you to address honestly?

  — What might you do to overcome those barriers?

  — What role could the development or strengthening of healthy boundaries play in overcoming those barriers to honesty?

Deeper Intimacy (page 126)

When Dennis and Christy were finally able to be honest with each other, the honesty made their connection real. From that point on, they established the connection they both longed for.

- Intimacy comes from "knowing" the other person at a deep level. If there are barriers to honesty, knowing is ruled out and the false takes over.

  — At what points, if any, could you identify with Christy's feelings? With Dennis's?

  — What, if anything, about how you feel in your marriage and about your desires for your marriage have you not yet been able to share with your spouse? How is your quietness on these matters inhibiting the development of deeper intimacy?

Couples often live out years of falsehood trying to protect and save a relationship, all the while destroying any chance of real relationship.

- We can't stress enough the importance of being able to share with each other your deepest feelings, needs, hurts, desires, failures, or whatever else is in your soul.

  — When has your spouse risked sharing with you some of the deepest feelings, needs, hurts, desires, failures, or secrets of his or her soul? Comment on how your relationship benefited.

— When have you risked sharing with your spouse some of your deepest feelings, needs, hurts, desires, failures, or secrets of your soul? Again, comment on how your relationship benefited.

— What feelings, needs, hurts, desires, failures, or secrets of your soul would you like to be able to share with your spouse? What is keeping you from doing so? What will you do to overcome those barriers or your own resistance?

If you and your spouse can feel safe enough in your marriage to be totally vulnerable, if you can help remove each other's fig leaves, then your marriage can take on some aspects of the state of paradise, such as vulnerability, safety, and intimacy. True intimacy is the closest thing to heaven we can know.

For a Reason (page 128)

Most of the time, in otherwise good marriages, deception takes place for "defensive" reasons. In other words, the dishonest spouse is often lying not for evil reasons, but to protect himself.

• For spouses to tell the whole truth, they must deal with their fears first.

— Which of the common fears listed on page 128 do you experience?

— What will you do to work through those fears? (The books *Changes That Heal* and *Hiding from Love* may help.)

- Review the six-point commitment—a total commitment to honesty— found on pages 128 and 129.

    — Which of these six points are already in place in your marriage?

    — Which of these six points need to be added or further developed? How will you do that?

    — If you are working through this book on your own, make a date with your spouse to talk about honesty in your marriage and review these six points. (In fact, you might want to make a series of dates, one per value!)

- Honesty not only involves speaking the truth. Honesty must be accompanied by enough grace to hear and deal with the truth it brings.

  — Are you able to deal with and accept the truth that your spouse might express to you? If you are, what enables you to hear the truth, accept it, and act on it?

  — If you are not yet able to hear the truth, what will you do to get to that point?

- Think back over the chapter. For what specific action, statement, effort, or attitude in regard to honesty can you affirm your spouse? Do so!

If you are to build a strong relationship, make a commitment of total honesty to each other. Talk with each other about how this value can become the bedrock of all that you do together, and then protect against deception and build on honesty.

Father God,

"I am the way and the truth and the life." Those were the words your Son spoke, and I see that the connection between truth and life is key. Almighty God, as you continue to work in my life, make me a person of truth in matters large and small, in deeds as well as words. May the presence of your perfect love in my marriage help cast out any fear I have about being totally honest with my mate. And, Lord, I ask you to make me a person who can hear the truth my spouse speaks so that our marriage will indeed—with your blessing—be a source of life to both of us. In Jesus' name. Amen.

Chapter 9

Value Four

Faithfulness

*T*rust. Confidence. Assuredness. Conviction. Fidelity. Truth. Certainty. Permanence. Rest. All of these words hint at what faithfulness is.

• A faithful spouse is one who can be trusted, depended upon, and believed in, and one in whom you can rest.

— Look again at the list of qualities that opens this chapter. Are you a faithful spouse? At what points do you feel weak?

— If you are ready to hear and accept truth (Value Three: Honesty), ask your spouse which traits you need to add or strengthen and then discuss how you might do that.

— What do you need to work on? What specific incident or habit do you need to apologize for and ask forgiveness for?

— On what points can you affirm your spouse's faithfulness? Affirm him or her for being faithful in those ways.

— At what points has your spouse not been faithful? Identifying those and facing them with honesty, love, and forgiveness is important to enjoying genuine intimacy in your marriage.

- The notion of faithfulness in marriage is too often shallow. We generally think of it only in the physical realm. Yet, in many marriages spouses are physically faithful but not emotionally faithful. Faithfulness means to be trusted in all areas, not just the sexual, to be trusted in matters of the heart as well as those of the body.

  — Can your spouse depend on you to deliver what you promise? To do chores faithfully as well as be sexually faithful? To stay within the monthly budget as well as come home when you say you will? To hear his or her heart without reprisal or condemnation? Which of these points—or which other behaviors where you are currently less than faithful—do you need to work on?

— On what points of faithfulness can you affirm your spouse? Let him or her know that you appreciate that faithfulness.

— Again, what do you need to work on? What specific incident or habit do you need to apologize for and ask forgiveness for?

• One of the words the Bible uses for trust (the Hebrew word *batach*) means to be so confident that you can be "care-less."

— Can your spouse depend on you to pick up the children from day care, bring home milk from the store, pay the bill, or make the appointment? What do you do to make your spouse "care-less"?

— Continue your words of appreciation to your spouse. Thank her for doing things that make you "care-less" because of her.

What Drives People Apart (page 131)

Faithfulness, of course, also means that you will not stray from the one you love. Physical adultery means giving yourself to someone else sexually. But you can commit emotional adultery as well; you can have an "affair of the heart."

- An affair of the heart means taking aspects of yourself and intentionally keeping them away from the marriage. (Remember that avoiding an affair of the heart does *not* mean that you cannot have deep, sustaining, healing, and supportive emotional relationships with other people.)

  — What aspects of yourself, if any, are you keeping away from your marriage? Consider what things you may be using to avoid your spouse. Is work, a hobby, or an addiction interfering? If you're not sure, your spouse may offer confirmation.

  — If something is interfering in your marriage, why are you letting it— and what will you do to make the necessary changes?

- Look again at Charlie and Leigh and the dynamic that had been driving them apart for several years.

  — How was each of them unfaithful to the other?

  — What, if anything, do you see about yourself in Charlie or Leigh?

"Objects" of unfaithfulness are numerous. Some are people, some are not. But the bottom line is that they come between you and your spouse. Some part of you avoids the relationship. This dynamic is about deliberately splitting yourself into two people, one of whom is not connected to the marriage.

No Excuses (page 134)

Many times one of the partners will justify unfaithfulness by the other's lack of safety. But an act of unfaithfulness is something done by one person, not two.

- God does not become unfaithful if we do not love him correctly. He remains faithful no matter what we do. Marriage requires this quality as well. Do not let your spouse's failures in love be an excuse for your unfaithfulness.

  — When has your spouse been faithful to you despite your failures in love?

  — What opportunities have you had—or what opportunity do you currently have—to be faithful to your spouse despite his or her failures in love?

- Different interests and different aspects of personal identity keep spouses from totally identifying with each other. One person cannot be all that you need in life.

  — What friends help round out your life? Give specific examples of interests they share with you that your spouse doesn't.

— What friends help round out your spouse's life? In light of what these friends offer your mate, are you as accepting of those friends as you could be?

• Think back over the chapter. For what additional action, statement, effort, or attitude in regard to faithfulness can you affirm your spouse? Do so!

It is never okay to use some lust to keep you split and keep you from integrating your heart to your marriage commitment. Such duplicity is taking your heart away from your marriage and bringing it somewhere else. This is unfaithfulness, in thought or in deed.

Lord,

Great is your faithfulness, even when I am not faithful. Teach me, I ask, to be faithful to my spouse—emotionally as well as physically—even when I am feeling disappointed, hurt, or unloved. And help me to "remain faithful until the end." Amen.

Chapter 10

Value Five

Compassion and Forgiveness

---

*T*he person you love the most and have committed your life to is an imperfect being. This person is guaranteed to hurt you and fail you in many ways, some serious and some not. You can expect failures to come.

- As the Bible says, "There is not a righteous man on earth who does what is right and never sins" (Ecclesiastes 7:20). We can expect failure from even the best people in our lives.

  — How do you tend to respond when your spouse lets you down?

  — How would you like to respond?

- What can you do when your spouse fails you in some way or is less than you wish him to be? Other than denial, there are only a couple of options. You can beat him up for his imperfections, or you can love him out of them.

  — The Bible says, "Love covers over a multitude of sins" (1 Peter 4:8). What are some of your sins that your spouse's love has covered?

  — What sins of your spouse could you choose to cover with love?

- "Nothing in a relationship has to permanently destroy that relationship if forgiveness is in the picture. No failure is larger than grace. No hurt exists that love cannot heal." Into what situation in your life, in your marriage, do these words speak hope?

For love to heal hurt and grace to prove itself stronger than failure, there must be compassion and tenderheartedness.

- What does *compassion* mean? *Strong's Hebrew and Greek Dictionary* describes God's compassion as "to bend or stoop in kindness to an inferior." For God to have compassion on our brokenness or sin is certainly to stoop to an inferior. But we need that same attitude toward an *equal* spouse for two reasons.

  — First, you forgive what is inferior to the ideal standard. You humble yourself to identify with your loved one, and you give up all demands for your spouse to be something he isn't at that moment. In what recent or even current situation would this perspective have helped you extend compassion to your mate?

  — Second, if your spouse is hurting or failing, you are not morally superior, but you are in the stronger position at that moment to be able to help. Again, in what recent or even current situation would this perspective have helped you extend compassion to your spouse?

- God never uses the stronger position to hurt, but always to help. And God calls us to "clothe yourselves with compassion, kindness, humility, gentleness and patience" (Colossians 3:12).

  — What does the verb *clothe* suggest about how we become compassionate, kind, humble, gentle, and patient?

— What will you do to be sure to be appropriately "dressed" the next time your spouse fails or is hurting?

If spouses "wore" the qualities of compassion, kindness, humility, gentleness, and patience whenever their mate failed or was hurting, we would see a lot more healed marriages. But that is not the human way. The human way is to harden our hearts when we are hurt or offended.

• Hardness of heart, much more than failure, is the true relationship killer (see Matthew 19:8). This is why the Bible places such a high value on tenderheartedness. And tenderheartedness consists of an identification with sin and failure; an identification with weakness; a willingness to become vulnerable again; and a willingness to repent.

— Review the discussion of these four elements of tenderheartedness (pages 138–39) and answer the questions in this checklist.

1. Do you have a familiarity with your own sins and therefore an attitude of humility toward your spouse's failures?

2. Are you dealing with your own pains and hurts, aware of your own vulnerabilities, and therefore able to have more empathy for your spouse, identifying with your spouse's weakness or inability as if it were your own?

3. Are you willing to be vulnerable again and trust your repentant spouse?

4. When you fail, do you own that failure and show a true change of heart and resulting change of behavior?

— What do your answers to these four questions show you about yourself? What steps toward being more compassionate and forgiving do you need to take? Be sure to involve God in this heart-changing process.

• Think back over the chapter. For what specific action, statement, effort, or attitude in regard to compassion and forgiveness can you affirm your spouse? Do so!

Compassion, tenderheartedness, and forgiveness ensure something very important. These qualities ensure that imperfect people can experience love and relationship for a long time. Clothe yourselves with them.

Loving God,

You call me to clothe myself with compassion, tenderheartedness, and forgiveness. I know I need to take responsibility, to choose to be compassionate, tender, and forgiving with my spouse. But I also know that I can't simply will myself, in my sinful nature, to be that way. I ask that you would be at work in me to make my compassion, tenderheartedness, and forgiveness a reflection of yours. I pray in Jesus' name. Amen.

Chapter 11

Value Six

Holiness

---

*H*oliness sounds stiff and boring to most of us. But in reality, holiness is attractive for a marriage.

- A holy person is someone who is "blameless." The Bible pictures holiness as not just being religious, but also being reality oriented. To be holy means to be pure and blameless. Because God is holy, his reality is ultimate reality. To the extent that we are not holy, we are farther away from the reality of life itself.

  — What new perspective on holiness—or what fresh reminder of what holiness is—did you gain from this discussion?

  — In light of the text's definition of holiness, why is holiness "attractive for a marriage"?

The equation is that God is life and ultimate reality and, therefore, for us to be unholy is a movement away from the ultimate reality of life.

- If every marriage placed value on holiness, at least five things would be present.

  — Which of these five are present, to one degree or another, in your marriage?

  Confession and ownership of the problems in each individual
  A relentless drive toward growth and development
  A giving up of everything that gets in the way of love
  A surrendering of everything that gets in the way of truth
  A purity of heart where nothing toxic is allowed to grow

  — What does this checklist suggest about what you can do to develop holiness in yourself and therefore in your marriage? Be specific.

- Consider again Kate and David's relationship. Until "holiness" was important to David apart from what Kate wanted from him, he was not truly holy.

  — On a scale of 1 to 10 (1 being "Why does it even matter?" and 10 being hungering for holiness the way a starving man longs for food), how motivated to be holy are you?

— The primary reason for growth must be that one is "hungering for righteousness"—not for someone else, but for oneself. Why do mixed motives mean the absence of true holiness?

David began to change when he realized how growing into the kind of person God wanted him to be was the best thing for him. Holiness began to have a different value to him besides "getting back into the house."

- Pursuing holiness means that you and your spouse pursue becoming the kind of people who can produce true love and life.

  — What might result in your person as well as your marriage if you wholeheartedly pursued holiness for the sake of holiness? Paint a picture, no matter how ideal it sounds, and remember that God can do far more than we ask or imagine (Ephesians 3:20).

  — What are you doing to pursue holiness—and what could you be doing? Be specific about your program and/or your plan.

- Think back over the chapter. For what specific action, statement, effort, or attitude in regard to holiness can you affirm your spouse? Do so!

Don't get holiness confused with some religious picture. Pursuing holiness means becoming whole. You become trustworthy, honest, faithful, and loving. In marriage, holiness is anything but boring. It is the kind of purity and trustworthiness from which the deepest kinds of passion flow.

Lord God,

As I consider whom you want me to be, I ask you to keep my heart soft toward you. Keep me submitting to you. May I be clay in your hands so I can be trustworthy, honest, faithful, and loving; so that I may be holy as you are holy. I pray in the name of your holy Son. Amen.

Part Three

Resolving Conflict in Marriage

Chapter 12

Three's a Crowd

Protecting Your Marriage from Intruders

Denise was in a funk, one that happened every year as her anniversary approached. Denise would think about her years of marriage to Roy as the day grew near. And she would become sad as she thought about what had happened to their union over the years. The couple's relationship revolved more around things and people than each other. Within her busy and fulfilling life, Denise often felt lonely and detached.

The Outside Affects the Inside (page 146)

Denise's situation illustrates an important aspect of boundaries in marriage: the marriage union itself needs to be actively protected. Many things compete for your love. You cannot assume that the strong connection you had when you first married will always "just be there."

- God designed both spouses to invest continually in their attachment to each other. Couples need to work to keep their love secure and safe.

  — On what points, if any, can you identify with Denise's feelings?

— What do you do, or could you do, to continually invest in your attachment to your spouse? To keep your love secure and safe?

• Marriage requires several kinds of boundaries to survive. We need to set limits on our individual needs, desires, and demands. We need to say no to our spouses. And we also need to have boundaries between the marriage and the outside world to preserve what we have. As stewards of the marriage covenant, you need to know how to structure your relationship so that the outside doesn't control what is inside.

— Review the list of intruders found at the bottom of page 146. Which ones threaten your marriage bond?

— "A marriage is only as strong as what it costs to protect it." Restate this in your own words and then use it as a gauge for evaluating your own marriage. On a scale of 1 to 10 (1 means "Nothing major has gone wrong, but the demands of life have caused us to grow apart; our marriage is in big trouble!" and 10 means "Our marriage requires constant, demanding work, but we are completely safe from intruders"), how strong is your marriage when it comes to standing against intruders? To what do you attribute its strength or weakness?

Like the man who sold all he had for the pearl of great price (Matthew 13:45–46), those who value the preciousness of their marriage will pay a high price to preserve it.

Why Two, Not Three (page 147)

Marriage is a two-person arrangement, leaving out all other parties. Marriage is meant to be a safe place for one's soul; third parties can become disruptive to this safety.

- **Triangulation**—One of the great enemies of good marriages, triangulation occurs when one spouse brings in a third party for an unhealthy reason.

  — Look again at the examples of triangulation (pages 147–48). Which situations, if any, remind you of your marriage?

  — Why is such triangulation painful, unjust, and destructive?

- What should you do if, right now or sometime in the future, you find that you are Person C, the one in the middle of two spouses?

- Marriage is designed to mature us. Living in such close proximity for so long with another person helps us come out of our isolation and self-centeredness. When has the heat you have experienced in your marriage resulted in growth? Be specific.

The effort to keep a caring connection for a lifetime would be impossible with the complexities of three involved. The only one who can do it perfectly is the Trinity!

Forsaking Is Protecting (page 149)

Most of us would like to avoid having to say no in life. It's work, it causes anxiety, and it can upset people. Yet reality dictates that in order to say yes to keeping a close marriage, you will have to say no to lots of other things.

- A life of yes to everything else ultimately results in a no to your marriage.

    — What recent decision was a yes to something else and a no to your marriage?

    — Why did you make that decision?

- Marriage means doing some hard work in forsaking, or leaving behind, other things.

    — Remember Linda and Tony? What, if anything, do you see about yourself (either as you are today or as you have been in the past) in Linda or in Tony?

    — All "intruder" problems are ultimately caused by either adding the wrong thing (inappropriate people or bad influences) to the marriage, subtracting the good (closeness and honesty) from the marriage, or both. What is your diagnosis of any "intruder" problems you are facing or have faced before?

Couples need to normalize the discipline of forsaking and make it a part of everyday life. "I need to check it out with my spouse" and "No, we need to spend some time together" are two of the best things any married person can say to protect his or her union from intruders.

When the Outside Isn't an Intruder (page 150)

When we address the idea of keeping out intruders, we are not saying that marriage is a self-contained unit in which each spouse meets every emotional need of the other. Marriage was not designed to be the source of all life for us. This would be idolatry.

- The marriage bond—a covenant between two adults—is one of God's many avenues of sustenance for us, along with his own love, the Bible, and relationships in the church.

  — Review the discussion of the parent-child dynamic that can appear in marriage (bottom of page 151). What, if anything, do you realize about your marriage as you read this description? More specifically, in what ways is one of you trying to re-parent the other?

  — If you have noticed a parent-child dynamic in your marriage, consider what to do to resolve that situation. Who in your life has God's interests and values in their hearts and can offer you the love, structure, or approval that you are not getting in a healthy way in your marriage? What might you do to foster a deeper connection with such people, or where might you go to find them?

Marriage simply does not have all the resources a couple needs. Because of this reality, we need outside relationships that can handle what the spouse cannot or will not.

- **A Word of Caution**—All good marriages need outside support, so we need to seek out the right and appropriate sources.

  — Now, in light of this caution, consider again the people you listed above as sources of support. Are they "for" your marriage? Are they playing the game of "poor you, being married to that bad person"? Basically, are these folks "right and appropriate sources" of help?

  — Good marriages need the support of people who are not only safe, but whose influence on us strengthens the marriage bond. If you have noticed that some of the people on your list don't meet these criteria, what will you do to move away from their "support"? Be specific in your plan and quick to act.

Your sources of love should not only be helping you but also be helping you love your mate.

The Intruder as a Symptom of Marriage Struggles (page 153)

Often the intruder isn't the issue. The intruder is the result, or symptom, of another issue in marriage. The real issue has more to do with your relationship or your character.

- Think back on Jerry and Marcia. Jerry felt he was being left out more and more by Marcia's schedule. Marcia, however, saw the problem as all those outside things that were besetting them. She felt like their victim.

— What, if anything, do you see of yourself in Jerry? In Marcia?

— If you found some similarities between yourself and Marcia, what issue in your marriage or yourself might your busyness be hiding?

- The very nature of marriage lends itself to allowing intruders inside the bond to disrupt it. Because nature abhors a vacuum, some distance (or vacuum) in the marital bond conveniently becomes filled with busyness. When a marriage contains conflict or hurt, we tend to busy ourselves in other people and activities.

  — Think for a moment about how busy you are. What indications, if any, do you have that it is an unhealthy busyness—unhealthy for you and/or your marriage? A close friend might help you evaluate your busyness.

  — When, if ever, have date nights and getaways (important to nourish a marriage) been disappointing because of unresolved conflicts?

  — What did you do—or, if the situation is current, what could you do—to bring the real issue to light and deal with it?

Activity can anesthetize the deficits and pain in the marital connection. When you become aware of this situation in your marriage, you need to bring the real issue to light and deal with it.

Intimacy Can Promote Intruders in Marriage (page 154)

The nature of emotional intimacy itself can make a marriage vulnerable to outside influences.

- When people spend a great deal of time together, the context of safety causes them to regress. They relax, feel more dependent, and act weak. Not only do couples regress, but they are also more exposed.

  — Which of these two side effects of intimacy have you experienced? In what areas of character and behavior, for instance, have you relaxed and regressed? Or when have you felt exposed in your marriage and threatened by that exposure?

- Intimacy causes two threats that leave the marriage open to intruders. The first threat is within ourselves. When we notice our vulnerability and exposure, we become frightened.

  — Which fear or guilt (listed at the top of page 155) have you experienced?

  — What were (or are) the ramifications for your marriage?

- The second threat to the marriage is not internal, but resides in the marriage relationship itself. When intimacy does its work, one spouse may pull away from what the other spouse reveals about hurts, failings, or sins.

  — When have you felt yourself pulling away from your spouse? Was it when he spoke about hurts, failings, sins, negative feelings, or certain aspects of himself?

  — What were, or are, the ramifications of that pulling away for your marriage?

- ***Filling the Vacuum***—When couples find that their intimacy is promoting intruders, it is best for them to take responsibility for the issue and begin to reconnect.

  — Why are the examples given in the text (page 156) encouraging?

  — Do you distance yourself from your spouse and his or her failings because withdrawal is the only boundary you have? If so, describe a recent incident and what you would have liked to have done differently.

— If you have trouble both staying connected and coming up with solutions to problems, what statement could you use to let your spouse know that you're having trouble being loving and truthful at the same time? Practice saying it aloud right now.

— What will you say if, when connection and solutions aren't happening at the same time, you notice your spouse being distant?

Spouses need to be both loving and truthful at the same time. This skill can help keep intimacy from promoting intruders.

Not Knowing Your Limits (page 157)

Often couples have problems with intruders because one or both of the mates simply are not aware of their own time, energy, and investment resources. The intruders win, and the couple loses.

• Consider Dale and Margaret's situation. What, if anything, do you see of yourself in Dale or Margaret? Give specifics from your own life to support your answer.

- In marriages like Dale and Margaret's, the "limitless" spouse is unable to see how his actions have consequences.

  — If you're like Dale to some degree, describe times when someone (your spouse) has rescued you from consequences of your irresponsibility. What current or imminent situation are you expecting to be rescued from or forgiven for? What would be a more responsible approach for you to take?

  — If you're like Margaret to some degree, why are you rescuing your spouse? Describe a recent situation and what you would do differently to help him or her learn from the consequences of irresponsibility.

Dale learned about the importance of limits from reality-based endings (the consequences of his actions) rather than happy endings (being rescued and forgiven), and his marriage improved.

Taking the Marriage for Granted (page 158)

A related issue in allowing intruders into a marriage occurs when one or both partners are unaware of the fragility of marriage. They tend to the crises or the squeaky wheels of work, parenting, church, and friends. The couple may also feel positive toward each other and so assume they are doing okay. This immature perspective on marriage can be a problem.

- Marriage is only as good as the investment people make in it.

  — What are you doing daily to invest in your marriage?

— What are you doing on a regular basis to invest in your marriage?

— What additional investments would strengthen your marriage? Be specific about what you will do and when you will take those steps.

- The marriage connection either deepens, opening both spouses up to the hearts of each other, or it starts to deteriorate, closing them off from each other. In light of that fact, we do not believe in an out-of-the-blue marriage problem.

  — Think about a problem in your marriage that you have overcome or one that you currently face. Looking back, what warning signs can you now see?

  — What calls for prevention—for being proactive in order to avoid a repeat of what you just described—do those warning signs suggest?

Do not mistake a lack of crisis as a sign that the marriage is healthy. Couples need to regularly check in with each other and ask the hard questions, such as "How do you feel about us?" and "What am I doing that hurts or bothers you?"

Problems in Setting Boundaries with Others (page 160)

Wade and Cindy's story is a common one. Wade didn't enjoy the intruders in his marriage and gave in to them grudgingly. He felt no freedom to choose and less afraid to let his spouse down than his boss or others. But this is a fatal error in perceiving safety.

- We should be able to trust a safe spouse and relax in her love. However, safety was never meant as a rationalization for neglecting the love obligation.

    — In what ways, if any, are you like Wade? If you see some similarities, what lessons can you learn from Wade's experience? How will you apply them in your marriage? Be specific.

    — In what ways, if any, are you like Cindy? If you see some similarities, what lessons can you learn from Cindy's experience? How will you apply them in your marriage? Be specific.

    — In what ways, perhaps different from Wade, are you neglecting the love obligation? What are you letting interfere with your commitment to your spouse and drain you of time and energy that should be invested in your marriage?

To take for granted that a spouse will "always be there for us" is, at some level, to place burdens upon that spouse's ability to love and trust us back.

- If fear and guilt are the reason your marriage has become infested with intruders, you need to refrain from nagging and threatening your co-dependent spouse. You also need to stay away from the tendency to ignore the problem and hope it goes away.

  — What nagging and threatening do you need to repent of and ask forgiveness for? What will you do instead when your spouse once again does or doesn't do that about which you are nagging and threatening?

  — What problem in your marriage, if any, are you ignoring? Review an example of what you could say to address your spouse about the problem (page 162) and adapt it to your specific circumstances.

Living in unconditional grace is never an excuse to be irresponsible or hurtful. If that is your spouse's approach to life, you need to maintain a position of love without rescue and of truth without nagging. Your own caring boundaries then provide hope for your spouse to develop his own sense of self and boundaries.

Inability to Live with Differences (page 162)

One thing we often hear from couples is that they feel distress over the differences between them. This section is about going outside the marriage because two people are different.

- The existence of separate friends and activities is not a red flag, but the tendency to be more invested in them than in the marriage is a red flag.

  — What red flags in your marriage, if any, does this statement help you recognize?

— Which friends and activities do you personally need to invest less in? (This is about *you* singular because you are the only one you can change.) In whom will you confide to hold you accountable and support you with prayer and encouragement?

• Being different should not be a problem in marriage. In fact, it should be a benefit (1 Corinthians 12:17–18).

— In what ways are you and your spouse different from one another? List five examples.

— Look again at your list. From which of these differences do you reap benefits? Explain those benefits.

• A couple's ability to deal with differences is a sign of their maturity. Grown-ups attempt to understand the other's viewpoint while holding on to their own reality.

— What does your approach to your differences suggest about the level of your maturity? Put differently, what opportunities for growth do your spouse's differences provide for you?

— Think back on a recent disagreement and honestly consider how hard you tried to understand your spouse's point of view. What does this look back help you realize about yourself and the dynamics in your marriage?

— The logical, obsessive husband learned to see his highly emotional and flighty spouse as spontaneous and fascinating. Which of your spouse's traits could you work on appreciating more?

Differences do not create intruder problems. Immaturity does. As spouses own their own weaknesses and issues, what used to drive them crazy often becomes a source of joy for them.

- **Conflict Avoidance**—Because you are not two clones, your differences guarantee conflict in marriage. Two people who feel strongly about how life should be lived will try to resolve the differences. However, some people fear conflict more than others do.

  — How was conflict regarded and dealt with in the home where you grew up? How has your background influenced your approach to conflict in marriage?

— Why is it wise to make conflict your ally?

— What step can you take toward making conflict an ally the next time you and your spouse disagree about something?

Again, make conflict your ally, not your enemy. It is the iron that sharpens your marriage (Proverbs 27:17).

The Intruders Themselves (page 165)

Having laid down the principles underlying intruder issues, we want to deal with some of the intruders that weaken the marriage bond and want to provide ways to guard against them. Remember that the intruders are a fruit, not a root, of the real problem.

- **Work**—Everyone is familiar with the stereotypical problem of the workaholic husband whose wife feels that he loves work more than her.

    — Is love of work a problem for you? If so, what issue may be behind it? See the possibilities listed on page 166.

    — Is love of work a problem for your spouse? If so, what issue may be behind it—and what can you do to help her deal with that issue? Again, see the situations listed on page 166.

In all of the scenarios described in this section, the answer is not to quit work, but to deal with the character and relational problems.

- **Friends**—It is common for couples to feel that friends have come between them.

  — Have friends become intruders in your marriage? If so, what issue— for either you or your spouse—may be behind that choice? See the possibilities listed on pages 166 and 167.

  — What can you do to resolve the issue(s) you just identified? Again, see the situations listed on pages 166 and 167.

Friends are a treasure in any marriage. As couples work on their issues, friends are not a boundary problem, but a gift that brings them closer.

- **Kids**—Children are built-in intruders on a marriage. They need so much, so often, from a couple. Yet the couple that puts parenting above their marriage has a problem.

  — What indications, if any, do you see in your marriage that the children are more important than the marriage relationship?

  — If you have let the priorities shift, what issue is behind that choice? And what can you do to resolve that issue? See the list on pages 167 and 168.

Remember that parenting is temporary and marriage is permanent, and live in light of that fact.

- **Affairs**—The most hurtful intruder—an affair—has been the death knell for many a struggling marriage.

  — If you or your (former) spouse has had an affair, what was the underlying problem? Possibilities are listed on pages 168 and 169.

  — What wake-up call did you hear in this discussion of affairs and the list of issues behind affairs?

We do not believe in automatically divorcing because of affairs. God simply permits, but does not demand, divorce in cases of adultery (Matthew 5:32). We have seen many cases in which affairs have led to greater intimacy and strength in the marriage.

- Work, friends, kids, and affairs aren't the only intruders. Parents, television, the Internet, sports, and shopping are others. These intruders need to be evaluated as to how they fit into the marriage, how they affect the less-involved spouse, and how to negotiate compromise so that both people can love and grow.

  — What intruders other than work, friends, kids, and affairs do you find interfering with your marriage?

  — What has caused you to let these intruders in?

— What will you do to control the intruder and create a situation in which you and your spouse can love and grow?

— What will you do to guard against the intruder(s) you just identified once you have dealt with the cause?

Even while you work on protecting your marriage from intruders, you will still have conflicts. The next chapter will help you deal successfully with the different types of conflicts that marriages face.

Lord God,

This chapter has reminded me again of both the gift and the challenge that marriage is—and I realize how much I need your help. Forgive me for neglecting my love obligation, for letting things interfere with my commitment to my spouse and draining me of time and energy that I should invest in my marriage. Help me to make that daily investment in my marriage, to make our differences be a source of joy, and conflict an ally. And, in order to keep our love safe and secure, help me to set and maintain boundaries between my marriage and the outside world. Protect us from intruders. Help me—help us—to say no to the things that intrude, things like busyness, work, friends, and kids—so that our marriage may be more what you intend it to be. In Jesus' name. Amen.

Chapter 13

Six Kinds of Conflict

onflict is not all the same. The rules are different for different kinds of conflict, but in most conflict there is not a right or wrong. In this chapter we want to help you distinguish what kind of conflict you are having. Then you may be better equipped to find a solution acceptable to both of you and to the relationship as well. We will examine six common marital conflicts.

Conflict #1: Sin of One Spouse (page 171)

In this simple scenario, there is a culprit. One spouse has sinned against the other. There is a true infraction, not an imagined one.

- There is no shortage of areas in which we can sin. In which of the areas listed in the first paragraph of page 171 have you fallen short of the glory of God?

- Humility and grace are the two most important attitudes that the Bible suggests in dealing with someone else's sin.

  — How did Jessica live out both humility and grace in dealing with Reggie's sin?

— Why is the path of humility and grace not a path of minimizing the sin?

Do not minimize the sin of your spouse, and ask him or her not to minimize yours. Go tough on the issue but soft on the person. Like Jesus, face sin with both grace and truth.

- Five steps for dealing with conflict involving the sin of one spouse are listed on page 173.

   — What do you appreciate about the steps described here? What is especially helpful?

   — Which step(s) will be hardest for you to implement? What will you do to overcome that difficulty?

   — How would you like to respond when and if your spouse needs to walk through this process in order to address your sin?

Couples need to take a hard stand against anything that violates their values. Again, go tough on the issue, but—as God does with you—go soft on the person.

Conflict #2: Immaturity or Brokenness of One Person (page 174)

All of us will fall short of the demands of life. This is a difficult concept for some people to understand. Most people who get married are totally unaware of their spouse's shortcomings.

- Remember Jerry and Genie?

  — Genie had some significant problems (such as depression and disorganization), and Jerry had some significant shortcomings in empathy and understanding. What immaturity or brokenness in you has your spouse had to deal with—or has to deal with now?

  — What immaturity or brokenness in your spouse have you had to deal with or do you have to deal with now?

In every relationship, the reality of the two people involved eventually surfaces. When it does, it is very important to face that reality—the immaturity, the brokenness—in the following helpful ways.

1. Accept Reality—Accept reality about yourself and your spouse. Both of you will be unprepared for some of the realities life brings.

  — What evidence of brokenness or immaturity have you seen in yourself? See the bulleted list on page 177. Why is recognizing this brokenness or immaturity important for your marriage relationship?

  — Why is it important to realize that none of the things listed are "sins"?

2. *Communicate Your Support to Your Spouse* —We do not grow when we are judged, nagged, condemned, resented, or subjected to some other lack of grace. We all need to feel that someone is on our side and supporting us (1 Thessalonians 5:14).

— What would you like your spouse to do to express his support of you? Does he know what words and actions make you feel supported? If not, when will you share that secret?

— In what ways do you effectively communicate your support to your spouse? If you don't know which of your efforts are most effective, ask your mate.

3. *Face Issues as Real Problems* —Part of love is honesty and requiring holiness and growth from each other. So, where your spouse is not mature, let her know.

— In what current situation, if any, can you follow the advice outlined in the second paragraph of page 178? Plan right now what you will say, and spend some time in prayer about the conversation you will have.

— How would you like to respond when your spouse approaches you about an area where you need to grow?

4. Own Your Problems—If you are the one confronted with your immaturity, own it. Be a "boundary lover."

— How do you usually respond to negative feedback?

— What would you like your response to be?

5. Get a Plan—We all need help, mentoring, support, and teaching. No one ever grew up on his own.

— In order to grow up, what person, professional, or organization can you turn to for help, mentoring, support, and teaching?

— What kind of resources, time, and energy might you need to devote to the problem?

6. Make It Mutual—Guard against labeling one spouse "the problem person." This is never true. Neither one of you is a complete person yet; you are both still growing up.

— Do you need to grow more in the relational area or in the functional area? Give evidence from your life to support your answer.

— What is behind any hesitation you may have in making the problems in your marriage mutual?

Equality and mutuality can solve a lot of problems if you are working as a team. Make the equality mutual, and make the problems mutual so that you can help each other.

Conflict #3: Hurt Feelings That Are No One's Fault (page 180)

Because we all have hurts and things to which we are sensitive, innocent things will set us off. What is important is that we learn how to deal with this kind of hurt where no one is really "wrong."

- What transpired between George and Mary was a familiar pattern in their relationship, and maybe it is for yours.

  — Review the bulleted list of steps in this pattern (pages 180–81). What interaction in your marriage, if any, does this remind you of? If it's a pattern in your marriage, which one of you (if either) tends to be more easily hurt? What may be behind that sensitivity?

  — Whether you are the one feeling hurt or the one unintentionally behind the hurt, what lesson did you learn from George and Mary?

Here are some hints for how to deal with hurt when no one is really "wrong."

1. When You Are Hurt, Acknowledge It to Yourself—Know yourself well enough to know when something is bothering you, and own your feelings.

— Why do you, if ever, ignore your feelings?

— Does your spouse tend to ignore feelings? What signals in your mate's behavior do you read as clues that he or she is hurt?

2. Communicate—Tell your spouse that you are hurt by something she did. But don't blame your spouse as if she has sinned.

— Is telling your spouse that you are hurt by something he or she did difficult for you? Why or why not?

— Why is the use of "I" statements wise and helpful?

3. Empathize—If you are on the other end of the hurt, show empathy for your spouse's feelings. Know that by caring and offering empathy you are not saying that it is your "fault."

— What opportunity do you have to be a healing agent for the hurt in your spouse's past? How do you want to deal with it? Feel free to share a situation you've already helped your spouse deal with as well as a current opportunity you have to do so.

— What hurts from your past have you shared with your spouse? How was he or she an agent of healing? Or what hurts from the past would you like to share with your spouse? What keeps you from doing so— and what will you do to remove those barriers?

4. Identify Patterns and Plan—Learn what hurts you. Then you can anticipate things that might hurt you in the future. Then you can take precautions to respond helpfully or, better yet, avoid the hurt altogether.

— What hurts you? What pattern do you see in the times in your marriage when you have felt hurt?

— Develop a plan to respond to the hurt next time it happens or, better yet, a plan to avoid the hurt altogether.

5. *Be in a Healing Mode* —We are all responsible for the hurts we carry around inside.

— When in your years of marriage, if ever, have you taken responsibility for a pattern of hurts you were feeling? What did you do, and what were the results of those actions?

— In what area of your life do you currently need to pursue healing? What will you do so that the hurt stops interfering in your life?

6. *Guard Against "Going to Court"* —George and Mary did what gets couples stuck: they tried to find out who was "wrong." Of course they never could, for no one was.

— Is it hard for you to not try to determine who was "wrong"? Why or why not?

— Why is not trying to determine who was "wrong" a good policy for your marriage?

Marriage is a place where old hurts inevitably get stepped on. But old hurts can heal as you respond differently to your spouse than he has been responded to in his "past life." Become a healing agent, with empathy, understanding, nondefensiveness, and care.

Conflict #4: Conflicting Desires (page 183)

Wherever you have two people, you will have conflicting desires.

- Two different people bring differences to the table. In fact, your differences are part of what brought you together. You complement each other.

  — Review the bulleted list on page 183. Where, if at all, do you see yourself and your spouse in this list? What are some other differences you can list?

  — Which of the differences you have noted were part of what brought you together? In other words, in what ways are those differences complementary?

Normally, two people develop a pattern of give and take, and differences get negotiated. But sometimes they hit a stalemate. A few principles can help.

1. Avoid Moralizing Your Preference—Humans tend to see what they prefer as right, especially if one of the preferences has a moral-sounding quality to it. Make sure you realize that your desire is not a higher one than your spouse's.

  — Which of your differences do you, or could you, easily moralize? Don't!

  — Why is this advice regarding conflicting desires wise? (Hint: When does moralizing ever lead to conflict resolution?)

2. *Empathize with and Understand the Importance of Your Spouse's Desires* — Avoid devaluing what your spouse wants. Validate her desires as real and good.

     — Which of your spouse's likes do you tend to devalue? What will you say instead the next time your spouse expresses a desire?

     — Which of your desires does your mate tend to devalue? What will you say the next time that happens?

3. *Move to Meet Your Spouse's Desires Before You Meet Your Own* — Seek to make sure that your spouse gets his or her desires met before yours are met, and you will avoid most arguments.

     — Think back on an argument. What desires were at stake? What could you have done to meet your spouse's desires? Would the argument have happened?

     — What would you like to be able to do and say the next time your desires conflict with your mate's?

4. If Necessary, Keep an Account of Yours, Mine, and Ours—If you keep an account, you will guard against the passive spouse becoming the perpetual loser. The more assertive one will finally get some limits.

— In what areas of life (such as spending or choosing) might you and your spouse benefit from keeping score? When will you start doing so?

— In what areas of married life would you do well to live more by the Golden Rule of doing unto your spouse as you would have him or her do unto you, a rule that preempts the need for keeping score?

5. Don't Define an "I" Choice as a "We" Choice—Make sure that when you want your spouse to do a "we" thing, he or she is really wanting to do that as well. If not, and he or she goes along, remember it is for you and not for the both of you. Count it in your own column.

— When have you defined an "I" choice as a "we" choice? What feelings, desires, or needs (feeling cheated if the other spouse wants to do something alone, not liking to be alone, etc.) were behind your behavior?

— When has your mate defined an "I" choice as a "we" choice? How did you respond—and how would you have liked to respond?

6. *Make Sure "We's" Are Agreed Upon*—Make sure you both sign off on activities that are really for the two of you. When you both have to sacrifice for something, make sure that you are on the same page in wanting it and agreeing to it.

— What grudge or emotional debt, if any, are you carrying because you never spoke up about your real feelings? What will you do about releasing that grudge or canceling that debt now?

— When, if ever, have you been surprised to learn from your spouse that he or she had not fully agreed to a "we"? How did you resolve that situation?

7. *Question Your Preferences*—Some of the things on which you take strong stances may not be true desires. As James tells us, we sometimes want things for wrong motives (James 4:3).

— Being busy, spending, competing in sports, working hard, serving— these activities may not be reflecting true desires. Think about your real preferences and any conflicts they generate in your marriage.

— Now check your motives for the preferences you just listed. What unhealthy issues, if any, are behind your choices and patterns? A trusted friend might help you answer this question.

8. *Expand and Grow*—Instead of fighting for your own way, give in to the preference of your spouse as a learning and stretching experience. Try to see the activity through your spouse's eyes, and you might learn to enjoy something you never thought possible.

— When, if ever, have you given in to your spouse's preference? What did you learn—or learn to like?

— What might you say to your spouse to encourage him or her to accept your preference as a learning and stretching experience?

Your marriage relationship can make you grow and expand if you let it. So let it!

Conflict #5: Desires of One Person Versus the Needs of the Relationship (page 189)

Sometimes the desire of one spouse conflicts with the needs of the relationship. And the problem comes when the marriage always serves one member and never the other. In the end, the marriage benefits as each member grows. But keep it in balance, making sure that the marriage gets served first.

• Remember the mother who is pursuing a talent and dream? Her family is pitching in and taking up the slack.

— When, if ever, have you sacrificed for your spouse, putting the marriage temporarily on hold? With what attitude did you approach that situation? In what ways did this experience strengthen or weaken your relationship?

— When, if ever, has your spouse sacrificed for you, putting the marriage temporarily on hold? With what attitude did your mate approach that situation? In what ways did this experience strengthen or weaken your relationship?

- Review the list of bulleted items on page 190. Which of these statements is a red flag for you? What warning—implicit or explicit—would you do well to heed?

Make sure that over the long haul the marriage goes on the back burner at times for each member and that each member has learned that the marriage is more important than his or her individual wants.

Conflict #6: Known Versus Unknown Problems (page 190)

We all have aspects to our personalities and character that we do not know about. As King David said, "Who can discern his errors? Forgive my hidden faults" (Psalm 19:12). David knew that there were things about himself that he did not know.

- In marriage, your spouse may know more about you than you do.

  — When, if ever, has your spouse seemed to know you better than you know yourself? Give a specific example or two.

  — In what ways, if any, do you seem to know your spouse better than he knows himself? Again, be specific.

— What conflicts, if any, has this knowledge of one another generated?

The trick to growth is becoming partner to this secret knowledge. There is a difference between known and unknown problems, however, and they should be handled differently.

- **Conflict in Known Problems**—What pointers about dealing with known problems (pages 191–92) are especially relevant for you and your spouse? To what current situation do you need to apply these pointers?

- **Conflict in Unknown Problems**—What ideas listed here do you find especially valuable? Why? When would they have been helpful in the past? Give an example, if possible.

In the next chapter we will deal with the process of how to solve conflicts with a spouse who supports the idea of boundaries.

Lord God,

I thank you that you are ever-present in this challenging relationship of marriage where conflict is indeed inevitable. I pray, Lord, for the grace to live by the Golden Rule; the courage to die to self and self-centeredness as I deal with conflict; the sense of humor and perspective necessary to keep me from majoring on the minors; and the awareness to call on you in prayer to grant me wisdom and patience, kindness and love as I seek to have you help me grow and mature through conflict. I pray in Jesus' name. Amen.

Chapter 14

Resolving Conflict with a Boundary-Loving Spouse

*S*hellie talked about Robbie's drinking, and she was also upset about his *workaholism. She seemed reluctant to agree to my (Dr. Cloud) seeing Robbie, saying she didn't think he would be very open to her complaints. But a few days later, when I went into the waiting room, she was sitting there with Robbie. I had braced myself for his denial, so it was refreshing to hear him say, "I have a problem. Please help me."*

Boundary Lovers (page 195)

I did not like Shellie and Robbie because their counseling issues were easy. I liked them because the process *was easy.*

- In any situation requiring change, two major issues appear right off the bat: (1) the issue to be dealt with, and (2) the ability of the person to deal with the issue. If number two is good, then in most cases, number one will not be a problem.

  — On a scale of 1 to 10 (with 1 being "Me? I don't have any problems" and 10 being Robbie or Shellie), how open to feedback and to the truth about yourself are you? Support your answer with evidence from your life.

— On that same scale of 1 to 10, how open to feedback and to the truth
   about himself is your spouse? Support your answer with evidence
   from your mate's life.

— To cement your answers to these two questions, review the traits of
   boundary lovers listed on page 196. Where do you see yourself need-
   ing to grow?

*People who are not open to feedback, cannot see when they are wrong, do
not like limits of any kind, and blame everyone else for their problems we call
"boundary resisters," and we will address them in the next chapter. But
people who have the ability to hear feedback and listen we call "boundary
lovers." If you have an attitude of openness, a desire for your spouse and
yourself to experience freedom and love, then you will be able to talk through
problems and help each other.*

An Overall Strategy (page 197)

*Conflict is normal. If you didn't have conflict, one of you would be un-
necessary in the relationship! In the previous chapter we discussed the six
different kinds of conflicts, giving numerous examples. For all kinds of conflicts, the Bible suggests the following predictable path.*

1. Observation—You can't fix a problem you do not see.

— Are you aware of a problem that your spouse does not yet see? Why
   have you been quiet about it?

— Could your spouse be aware of a problem that you don't yet see? How would you like to respond if and when your mate brings it up? What will you do to invite that discussion?

2. Confrontation—You can't fix a problem you don't talk about.

— When have you been slow to talk with your spouse about a problem? How did your hesitation impact the problem and your relationship with your spouse?

— Using either a hypothetical problem or one you currently face in your marriage, practice now speaking the truth to your spouse and doing so in love. What will you say, and how will you say it?

3. Ownership, Grief, and Apology—If you are the problem—or at least part of it—own it. If you have been hurt, own your hurt and communicate it. If you are the one who is doing the hurting, then confess and apologize. If you are the wounded party, forgive as well as express your hurt.

— Into which category—being hurt or doing the hurting—do you currently fall? According to this list (page 198), what should you do— and when will you do it?

— When have you *not* acted according to this formula of ownership, grief, apology, and forgiveness? What impact did your actions have on your marriage relationship?

4. Repentance—Once you see your part in something, repent.

— When has your "repentance" been merely a matter of words? What impact did this pseudo-repentance have on your relationship with your spouse?

— Genuine repentance requires action: a change in direction, a change in behavior. What repentance, if any, do you need to be living out now? Be specific about the actions you will take to do so.

5. Involvement in the Process—Problems do not go away immediately. Become involved in whatever process will be necessary for change.

— Think back on a problem you and your spouse have encountered. Describe the process of change involved in resolving the problem. What did that process demand of you? Be specific. What might have happened in your marriage had you not gotten or stayed involved in resolving the problem?

— What current problem in your marriage will challenge you to get and stay involved in the process of resolving it? What will you do to be sure you persevere?

6. Reexamination—Have some system of reexamination. Get a checkup from those to whom you have made yourself accountable. And then continue to get reexamined for other things as well.

— Consider past problems in your marriage. Give an example of one that recurred to some degree. What might have prevented that recurrence?

— Who can reexamine you for any recurrence of a past issue? When will you talk to that person/those people? What benefits do you think will come from such reexamination?

If you have a boundary-loving spouse and are one yourself, you are fortunate indeed. It means that you are open to truth, responsibility, freedom, and love. And if both of you are open to such things, God will help you find them.

• Conflict can still be painful even if everyone is open to feedback. Negative things hurt, and losing things hurts as well.

— Review the basic rules of communication (pages 198–99). Which ones, if any, do you tend to break? In light of these violations, what growth needs to take place?

— Despite the admonition "Above all, don't be afraid of conflict," are you still afraid of conflict? Why? What will you do to grow past that fear? (Our books *Hiding from Love* and *Changes That Heal* can give you some ideas.)

Again, don't be afraid of conflict. There is always a death before a resurrection and conflict before deeper intimacy. Go through it lovingly, and chances are you will find more intimacy with your mate on the other side.

In the next chapter we will see what conflict looks like with someone who is not so open to boundaries.

Holy and heavenly Father,

Help me to see problems I need to address, and then to speak about them in truth and love. Enable me to own the problems I need to own, to own any hurt I may feel, to confess and apologize when I'm hurting my mate, and to forgive my mate when I'm the one being hurt. Strengthen my resolve to truly repent, to change my actions and not just say the words. Grant me the ability to persevere. Fill me with the grace I need for times of reexamination as well as times when my mate and I are working on our marriage. Also, Lord, may your Spirit work in me so that I can seek to understand my mate before seeking to be understood; actively empathize with my spouse; and listen instead of rushing to defend myself. Make me more like Christ. In whose name I pray. Amen.

Chapter 15

Resolving Conflict with a Boundary-Resistant Spouse

*M*ichael and Sharon got into real financial trouble and almost lost *their home. During this difficult phase, a friend told Michael, "You're working on the wrong problem, Michael. It's not that you don't make enough money. Your problem is that you don't understand that Sharon doesn't like to hear the word no." That diagnosis changed everything. They could start working on how Sharon hates limits and how Michael is afraid to set them with her.*

- At the root of Michael and Sharon's financial troubles was a boundary issue: a resistance to accepting limits. What conflict in your marriage might actually be a boundary issue? Explain.

Boundaries Aren't Always Welcome in Marriage (page 201)

Michael and Sharon illustrate a difficult reality: boundaries aren't always welcome in a marriage. But that is not how God intended it. God designed boundaries for some very good reasons, all of which benefit a couple.

- Boundaries protect love. They enhance freedom. They allow people to be separate and stay connected. They define responsibility so that people know what their tasks are. Boundaries operate best when both spouses restrict their freedoms so as to better love each other.

  — What legitimate freedoms do you curb so as not to hurt your mate? What tendency to be selfish do you fight against in order to love your spouse? Give an example of one or both of these situations.

  — What freedoms do you see your mate not exercising so as not to hurt you? What tendency to be selfish do you see your spouse fighting against in order to love you? Again, give an example of one or both of these situations.

- Love can only flourish and deepen when two people embrace the pain of receiving and respecting their mate's boundaries.

  — Which of the following have you experienced as you have respected your spouse's boundaries or had him respect yours? Explain.

  More compassion for your spouse's needs, desires, and hurts
  Greater self-control and patience
  Humility and the ability to correct yourself
  An appreciation of your mate for who he is, not for his usefulness to you
  Greater dependence on your own values to make you happy; less dependence on your spouse for your happiness

— What have you learned about how God respects our boundaries with him, from this study of boundaries and/or your real-life experiences with boundaries?

• For people who control others or who don't take ownership of their lives, the boundary message doesn't come as good news or something that brings freedom.

— Is the boundary message good news for you? Why or why not? Be specific and honest about who you are.

— Controlling spouses need to hear that they are hurting someone they love. They need to hear that things need to change, and change is difficult and often painful. What changes (listed on page 203) will be hard for you or your spouse?

Accepting boundaries hurts sometimes. It is realistic to identify pain as pain, even if it is growth-producing pain. The painful discipline of boundaries will eventually bear good results in our lives (Hebrews 12:11). And we believe that boundaries are the only way to keep love alive.

Character Is What You Do with the Pain of Boundaries (page 204)

Good character welcomes the pain of boundaries, as a person of character wants to love God and others and grow spiritually and emotionally. A person of problem character, however, refuses to accept his status as someone who sometimes needs correction and limits from others.

- There are many "mixed marriages"—mixed in terms of the spouses' views of boundaries. It is sad when one spouse finds that the other is not willing to carry his load.

  — Is yours a "mixed marriage"? Explain why you answered as you did.

  — Which example of a mixed marriage (listed on pages 204–5) is most similar to yours?

In mixed marriages, one spouse has too much responsibility, and the other has too little. Also, the boundary-busting spouse is refusing to make the right changes.

How the Boundary Buster Sees the Issue (page 205)

The boundary-loving spouse doesn't understand the perspective of the boundary-resistant one. She is often surprised or shocked to learn how differently her spouse thinks and feels. And, since you are reading this chapter, we are assuming that you are the boundary-loving spouse. You should find the remainder of the chapter very helpful.

- People who don't respect others' boundaries have a basic attitude toward life: I should be able to do what I want.

  — What evidence have you seen in your marriage that your spouse feels he should be able to do what he wants?

— What evidence do you see in other areas of his life that your spouse feels he should be able to do what he wants?

• What conflicts (past or present) in your marriage have been exacerbated by your spouse's sense that he should be able to do what he wants? Give a specific example or two.

The boundary-resistant spouse feels that he should be able to do whatever he wants whenever he wants. With that as his operative principle in life, he will challenge and protest any boundary until he begins to grow up. Boundaries say that you cannot do what you want all the time.

Ignorance Is Not a Character Problem (page 206)

We are not saying that all boundary-busting spouses have a character problem. Many times what appears to be selfishness is actually ignorance.

• Your spouse may be crossing boundaries with you out of a lack of awareness. So approach the problem first as an ignorance issue.

— In what area does your spouse tend to cross boundaries with you?

— What evidence do you see, if any, that he or she is unaware of your boundaries (that is, desires)?

— When and how will you let your spouse know that his or her behavior is hurtful or irritating?

— How do you expect your mate to respond to what you say—and how do you want to respond to each of those possible reactions? Plan— and pray—ahead.

When you tell your spouse that he has crossed your boundaries, either your spouse will love you for telling him (Proverbs 9:8) and will make the changes, or he will resist it. And this resistance is a bigger problem.

The Spouse of the Boundary Buster Needs Scrutiny (page 207)

Discovering that your spouse is a boundary buster doesn't mean he is any worse a person than you are. Beware of judging and condemning (James 2:13).

- One way to be merciful to your boundary-resistant spouse is to look honestly at your own sin.

  — Which of the actions and attitudes listed on pages 207 and 208 do you need to repent of and ask your spouse's as well as the Lord's forgiveness?

— When will you ask your spouse to forgive you for the sins you just ac-
knowledged?

*You can see why you may have to carve out time to work on setting
boundaries, as it takes so much time to deal first with ourselves.*

Causes of Boundary Resistance (page 208)

*Before you address the problem of the boundary-resistant spouse, you
need to understand the reasons for boundary resisting to help you know better how to approach the issues.*

- ***Empathic Failure***—Some people have difficulty becoming aware of
  their effect on people. They have trouble sensing emotionally that they
  hurt others. This is a problem in compassion.

  — What evidence of this reason for boundary resisting do you see in
  your spouse?

  — What could you do to open up the world of emotions and relationships to this spouse?

- *Irresponsibility*—None of us takes responsibility for ourselves grace-fully. But some spouses have a low sense of ownership of their actions. They feel that they should be able to do whatever they want and suffer no consequences for it.

  — What evidence of this reason for boundary resisting do you see in your spouse?

  — What might help your spouse see that she is the major cause of her problems?

- *Inability to Receive Limits and Stay Free*—A spouse may resist boundaries because of a split within his own soul. He may be unable to receive confrontation or consequences due to a lack of integration of love and freedom.

  — What evidence of this reason for boundary resisting do you see in your spouse?

  — What could you say to your spouse to help him see how to preserve his freedom within certain boundaries?

- **Control of Others**—Some spouses resist boundaries due to their attempts to control, manipulate, or dominate their mate. They are unable to see their spouse as having separate and equal feelings and ideas. Believing that their way is the only way, they negate and minimize the freedom of their spouse.

  — What evidence of this reason for boundary resisting do you see in your spouse?

  — A person with the problem of control sometimes needs love, confrontation, and consequences. What could these three steps look like in your marriage?

- **Denial of Imperfection**—Spouses who refuse to admit weakness and fault can be major boundary busters. They try to avoid owning their fault or sin.

  — What evidence of this reason for boundary resisting do you see in your spouse?

  — What kind of consequences might help your spouse learn to admit weaknesses and fault? And where could your spouse go to safely explore his "bad parts"?

- **Retaliation**—Sometimes a marriage can be troubled by a spouse who takes revenge on perceived or real transgressions by his mate. When he feels wronged, he feels justified in more wrongdoing: an eye for an eye. This can cause tremendous boundary problems.

  — What evidence of this reason for boundary resisting do you see in your spouse?

  — Where can you take your hurt feelings so you can heal? What can you do to protect yourself from retaliation? What can you do to solve the problem rather than take revenge?

- **Transference**—The intimacy generated by marriage can revive old feelings toward other significant relationships. The confusing state of having feelings toward a spouse that are about someone else is called *transference*.

  — What evidence of this reason for boundary resisting do you see in your spouse?

  — How might you help your spouse see that transference happening?

- ***Specific Context of Resistance***—Some spouses are empathic, humble, correctable, and respectful of boundaries in all areas but one. These context-specific situations can cause a great deal of distance in an otherwise loving marriage.

  — What evidence of this reason for boundary resisting do you see in your spouse, and what might be causing that resistance? Some possibilities are listed on page 214.

  — The context of boundary resistance may signal a need to look more deeply into the marriage and the hearts of the spouses. What will you do to take that closer look at your marriage as well as your own heart?

The presenting problem is rarely the real problem. So again, you need to understand the reasons for boundary resisting to help you know better how to approach the issues.

If It Is Character, You Have a Job to Do (page 215)

Let's suppose your spouse is aware of your feelings and concerns, but ignores, minimizes, or otherwise resists your boundaries. If this is your situation, you have some work ahead of you. In this section we want to give you a structure to follow to help deal with your resistant-spouse problem in a caring, yet truthful manner.

- You must not approach this problem as if you are a team. At this point, you have an adversary. Why is it important to keep this fact in mind?

- Review the list of "Don'ts" found on pages 215 and 216. Which of these will be hardest for you *not* to do? Call on the Lord for his help.

Like a child having a tantrum, your spouse may hate you for entering the world of boundaries. So understand that you are on your own, within the marriage, in approaching the issue. But you do have God and your boundary-loving friends.

Your To-Do List (page 216)

The following specific principles of operation will give you a way to approach your boundary-resistant spouse with grace and truth.

- **Make Soul Connections**—Your hopes to fulfill your God-given need for love may be jeopardized when you set boundaries with your spouse.

    — Who in your life serves as a resource for comfort, encouragement, and strength—things you will need during the stress of boundary negotiation with your spouse?

    — Or where can you go to find good folks to open up to and to find support for your boundaries? (See our book *Safe People* for tips.)

- ***Grow and Own***—It makes sense that if you try to help a difficult spouse learn about love and responsibility, you will grow in these capacities as well. Also, you become free to grow the moment you realize that to some extent you have contributed to the problem.

  — Whether working through *Boundaries in Marriage* is your first step or just one of many you have taken toward healthier boundaries, what personal growth have you noticed so far?

  — What have you learned about where you need to be growing?

- ***Identify the Specific Issue***—Once you are connected and in the boundary-setting process, you will need to find out what the specific boundary issue is.

  — If possible at this point, describe the following aspects of the issue:

    What boundary of yours is being violated?
    How is that violation affecting you and your love for your spouse?
    Is the problem a pattern or an occasional event?
    Is it important enough to risk conflict? Why or why not?

— Are you asking your spouse to change her heart or simply her behavior? Are you asking for a character change or a boundary change? Why have you made that decision?

- *Validate Your Spouse*—Resistant spouses still need to know that you understand their perspective. People have a difficult time changing when their feelings are negated and dismissed.

  — In what ways—verbal or nonverbal, consciously or otherwise—do you negate or dismiss your spouse's feelings? Your spouse can help you answer this question if you're not sure.

  — What kind of validation (see bulleted examples on page 221) have you offered, or could you offer, your spouse?

- *Love Your Spouse*—In boundary conflict resolution, you need to communicate that your goal is to be close to your spouse, not to hurt him. Boundaries are about protecting love.

  — How has your spouse responded to your attempts to resolve boundary conflicts? What does that reaction tell you about his perception of what you're doing and why?

— Describe your current boundary conflict in terms which show that, in your attempts at resolution, your goal is love.

- **Create a Level Playing Field**—Here is some hard news: you have to earn the right to require your spouse to change.

    — In what ways, if any, are you contributing to the conflict in your marriage?

    — Ask your spouse about your contribution to the boundary conflict. Ask honest and safe friends. And ask God to search your heart (Psalm 139:23–24).

- **Request Change**—You are responsible for stating the boundary problem and your request for change.

    — Draft your request for change.

    Let your spouse know about your love: _____

    Let your spouse know about your own faults: _____

    Be clear and specific about your request: _____

— What responsibility are you transferring to your spouse by following the three-step approach just defined?

• ***Give Your Spouse Time and Patience***—Make the request and allow some time to observe her response.

— When have you seen time help a healing process? Be specific.

— What evidence have you seen that your spouse needs time to adjust to the new reality of a mate with boundaries?

• ***Establish Appropriate Consequences***—Stating your boundary may not be enough. Whatever your spouse is doing that is hurting you, the benefits he receives may far outweigh your appeals and requests. At this point, you need to set consequences.

— When have consequences helped you learn something important and contributed to the growth of your character? Be specific.

— Review the list of important characteristics of consequences (page 225) as well as the chart that follows (page 227). Now define what consequences—what discomfort due to irresponsibility—might be appropriate to establish and allow in your marriage situation.

- ***Warn Your Spouse***—If you have requested change and have given time with no result, your spouse needs to be aware that you will now begin setting limits.

  — Why will your situation benefit from such a warning?

  — If your request for change and some time for healing don't bring about the desired results, plan and perhaps even practice delivering—with grace and truth—the warning you may need to give your spouse. Be sure you're clear that you don't want to trap or punish him. You don't want him to suffer; you just want the problem solved so that you may reenter love.

- ***Follow Through***—A boundary without a consequence is nagging. Be sure to follow through with the limit you have set.

  — What might keep you from following through on consequences with your mate? Some possibilities are guilt, fear of loss of love, and fear of your spouse's escalating behavior.

— What will you do to overcome those obstacles to following through?

- ***Observe and Evaluate Over Time***—Again, let time pass before you follow through with consequences.

  — What kind of support will you have—or look for—while you wait to see how quickly your spouse will recognize her irresponsibility or selfishness?

  — What different consequences might you establish?

- God grieves with you when a spouse continually resists the boundaries of love.

  — How can the freedom to be selfish and hurtful sometimes be the freedom through which some people eventually choose God's ways? Give an example from real life.

  — Read the C. S. Lewis quote again (page 229). Why is free will—which can be the cause of pain and evil—also "the only thing that makes possible any love or goodness or joy worth having"?

Even if your spouse is very boundary resistant at this point, understand that your boundaries are more for you than for your spouse. They are to protect and structure you, and only secondarily to change and motivate him.

Deal with Escalation and Anger (page 229)

Don't be surprised or shocked if your spouse escalates the behavior that troubles you. Be prepared for this. Warn again and make the consequences stricter, or simply make sure you are sticking to them consistently.

- Many spouses back off an appropriate boundary they have set because they can't tolerate being hated.

  — Who else in your life can fill you up with love and support when you're not receiving that from your spouse?

  — What are you doing to stay connected to God? To other people?

Allow the hatred to exist. Your spouse has the right to hate your no. Just understand where it comes from, don't react to it, and stay connected to God and others.

Normalize Doubt (page 231)

Don't be surprised if you begin questioning yourself.

- You may doubt whether your boundary setting is the right thing to do.

  — Which of the questions listed on page 231 have you asked yourself since trying to establish healthier boundaries in your marriage to a boundary-resistant spouse?

— What is your answer to each of these questions—today?

Setting limits with your soul mate is a serious endeavor. At the same time, realize that any new way of operating in life is accompanied by doubt. Expect it. Settle the question, and continue the process.

Leave Permanently (page 231)

It is sad but necessary to bring up the ultimate consequence in marriage: divorce. Divorce can only be the last step in a long process that includes prayer, invitation, change, patience, consequences, and love.

- Look again at your boundaries and the consequences you have established. Are they constructed so that you aren't the one leaving, so that your righteousness and God's painful realities will force your spouse over time either to relent or to change? Support your answer with specifics.

This chapter has dealt with some difficult realities about setting boundaries with a spouse who does not support boundaries. Yet, remember that God supports you as you follow his ways. Cling to him and your friends as you establish good limits for you and your marriage.

Lord God,

You are the Author of love and my Creator. I pray that you will fill me with your love for my boundary-resistant spouse. May your Holy Spirit help me live out the Golden Rule in my marriage. And may my roots in you grow deep so that I can stand strong when my spouse's behavior is hurtful. Also, I ask you to keep me very aware of my sin, of my need for you, so that I might be merciful and forgiving toward my spouse, not proud and arrogant. And, Lord, grant me patience as this boundary-building process unfolds. May I trust in your timing even as I turn to you for guidance and wisdom and hope. Enable me to persevere and, I pray, give me your love and compassion for my mate. In Jesus' name. Amen.

Part Four

Misunderstanding Boundaries in Marriage

Chapter 16

Avoiding the Misuse of Boundaries in Marriage

Boundaries were not designed to end relationships, but to preserve and deepen them. With couples, boundaries are ultimately for working within the marriage, not outside of it. Misuse of boundaries often results in increased alienation instead of increased love.

- Take a moment for a brief self-check. Are you working on boundaries in order to preserve your marriage and increase love, or to justify wrong and unloving behavior?

The purpose of this chapter is to clarify some misconceptions about boundaries in marriage. We will look at the purpose of suffering, how boundaries fit into problem solving in marriage, the issue of submission, and the divorce question.

The Purpose of Suffering (page 236)

Remember Riley and Emily? Riley's struggle is an example of the problem of thinking that setting boundaries means we don't have to suffer. But boundaries are not about an escape from suffering, nor an escape from responsibility. In fact, when we set limits in marriage, sometimes we suffer more, not less.

- Suffering, at least the kind God has called us to experience, is designed to help us adapt to reality the way it really is.

  — What lessons have you learned in the school of suffering? What reality has suffering helped you adapt to? Give an example or two, being specific about the lesson and how you learned it.

  — What lessons have you learned from any hurt you have experienced in your marriage? What reality has that suffering helped you adapt to? (Some benefits of suffering in marriage are listed on pages 237–38.) Again, give an example, being specific about the lesson and how you learned it.

Suffering helps us survive, even thrive, while giving up the wish to be God.

- What new perspective does this discussion of suffering give you on a current issue in your marriage? In other words, what lesson can you be learning from the present struggle or pain?

Almost all of the processes that strengthen and deepen a marriage involve some pain and discomfort. Suffering pushes us into the learning curve of adulthood.

Suffering for the Wrong Reasons (page 238)

Confusion about suffering, boundaries, and marriage often comes, not because spouses try to avoid growing up, but because they have been suffering for some time for the wrong reasons. Godly suffering is good for us, but ungodly suffering is not.

- Ungodly suffering comes from either doing the wrong thing or not doing the right thing.

  — When have you experienced ungodly suffering in life? What wrong were you doing or right were you not doing? Did the ungodly suffering resolve itself when you stopped doing whatever caused it? Explain.

  — When have you experienced ungodly suffering specifically in your marriage? Again, what wrong were you doing or right were you not doing? Did the ungodly suffering resolve itself when you stopped doing whatever caused it? Explain.

- Godly suffering changes as we grow. We keep suffering as we mature in different tasks. The compliant spouse speaks up and tells the truth. This is difficult for her; it is godly suffering. But as she matures in truthfulness, she realizes she has a judgmental, condemning spirit. So she begins to work on forgiveness and compassion to resolve that problem. That, too, is godly suffering.

  — Think about your own experience. When have you experienced different types of godly suffering as you worked through the different levels of the same issue? For instance, like the once-compliant woman just described, what issue are you currently revisiting on a deeper level? Describe what the suffering was like earlier and what it is like now.

- God does not want you to set boundaries in your marriage to end suffering and pain. He wants you to end the ungodly suffering, which produces no growth, and enter *his* suffering, which always brings good results.

  — Review the table found on page 240. Which situation parallels something in your marriage? Are you experiencing godly or ungodly suffering as a result of that situation? What does the table suggest you do if you are suffering the wrong way?

If you are going to endure discomfort, you may as well have it do some good. Don't set limits to live an anesthetized life. Set them to build love, honesty, and freedom in your marriage.

Setting Boundaries to Avoid Growth (page 240)

Remember Vicki and Colton? Vicki didn't understand that boundaries are not a simple ultimatum. Colton had no chance to feel her love or concern, only her wrath. So he did what most of us do when we feel anger but no love from someone: he became angry back. That is when everything fell apart.

- Boundaries involve more than just issuing ultimatums that set limits. Both spiritual and emotional growth require a complex set of situations. It takes a lot for us to mature.

  — When, if ever, have you been given an ultimatum that communicated the basic message "Grow up!"? Did that ultimatum prompt growth? Why not?

  — When have you given your spouse an ultimatum? Was it effective in helping her grow up and change? Why not?

- *Love*—When problems arise in marriage, the first thing to do is to establish that you desire the best for your mate, even if he has not been a loving person himself.

  — Does your mate clearly understand that you desire the best for him? If so, what did you do to establish that fact in his mind?

  — If not, what will you do to make it clear that you are working on boundaries because you desire the best for him?

  — If you are not sure your spouse understands that you want the best for him, when will you ask your spouse if he feels loved even as you set boundaries?

- *Others*—Not only do you need to speak from love, but also you need to be receiving care, support, and encouragement from God and others outside your marriage.

  — With whom outside your marriage are you connected? From whom are you receiving the care, support, and encouragement you need as you do this important boundary work in your marriage?

— What are you doing to stay connected to God as you work on boundaries in your marriage? What might strengthen that connection?

- **Ownership**—There are almost no marriage problems in which one spouse contributes one hundred percent and the other, zero percent.

  — Step back from your marriage or ask a close friend for a more objective perspective. What have you contributed, or are you contributing, to the boundary issues in your marriage?

  — What can you do to own the problem, take responsibility for it, and improve the situation? Also, how does this ownership change your attitude toward your spouse?

- **Invitation**—Whatever the problem between you and your spouse, invite him to change before you set limits. With empathy and love, request that he make a change. Invitation can preclude having to set some consequence.

  — What would be an appropriate invitation for you to extend to your spouse right now?

— Exactly what will you say—and how will you say it? Your delivery is key!

- **Warning**—When we warn our spouse, we tell him that something painful might happen in the future and that his behavior will help determine what happens.

  — Assuming your spouse does not accept your invitation to change, what warning will you give her?

  — What "something painful . . . in the future" would be a logical or natural consequence for her unchanging behavior?

- **Patience**—Silent suffering is not patience. Patience allows the process to happen while you are providing love and truth, the ingredients of growth.

  — In what efforts to change have you personally experienced God's patience?

— In response to God's patience with you (2 Peter 3:9), what will you do to show your spouse patience, to be loving and truthful, while you allow him time to grow? Be specific about what you will stop and what you will start doing and saying.

- **Consequence**—When love, support, invitation, warning, and patience are in place, you may have to follow through on your consequence. Consequences protect you and also help your spouse deal with the reality of his actions.

  — Boundaries should not grow out of anger, revenge, or punishment. Have yours? A close friend may offer you a reality check.

  — In what relationship(s) will you find the strength you need to be consistent as you enforce boundaries with your spouse?

- **Renegotiation**—Many boundaries can be changed over time as a spouse matures and changes. What you make external can become internalized in your marriage, as it becomes a part of who you two are.

  — What boundaries, if any, have you renegotiated through the years as you and your spouse have grown?

— The more people grow, the fewer rules they need. When have you seen this to be true in real life, perhaps in your own life or in the lives of children?

— In marriage, try to operate with as few rules as possible. Why is this good advice?

• *Forgiveness*—Finally, be actively and constantly in the process of forgiveness. To forgive is to cancel a debt. You need to both forgive your spouse and request forgiveness from your spouse.

— Setting boundaries involves risks that can disrupt the process of marriage growth. Which disruptions listed on page 245 do you tend to bump up against in your marriage? Why?

— What will you do to more consciously and more genuinely live in forgiveness? What, for instance, might become a regular prayer?

When God wants to help us grow, he does more than simply set a limit. He uses his boundaries as one of several elements to encourage us to change, mature, and become what he intended us to be. The process of growth is difficult, but the alternative—divorce—is worse.

But before we talk about divorce, let's take a brief look at how the idea of submission in marriage has been misused.

Submission (page 246)

Few passages in the Bible have been subject to more misunderstanding and misuse than Ephesians 5:22–23, 25. It has, for instance, been used by a husband wanting to control and not serve his wife.

- What new understanding of Ephesians 5:22–23, 25 do you have after reading the discussion on pages 246–48?

- What greater appreciation for God's plan for marriage do you have after reading this Ephesians passage?

- Focus on yourself—the only person you can change—and not on your spouse. What changes in yourself—in your attitudes, actions, words—does this Ephesians passage suggest need to be made?

Leadership does not mean domination. Marriages that work best have equal, interdependent partners with differing roles. The idea of submission is never meant to allow someone to overstep another's boundaries.

- A leader is a giving servant who is committed to the best of the one(s) he or she is leading. If a wife is resisting a husband who is loving, truthful, protective, and providing for her well-being, then something is wrong.

  — If you are a husband, are you loving, truthful, protective, and providing for your wife's well-being? What can you do to improve on these counts? Be specific—and then act!

  — If you are a wife, are you resisting your husband in some area? What can you do to be in accord with God's design? Be specific—and then act!

If you and your spouse are not using your freedom and boundaries to give to and to serve each other, then you do not understand love. As Paul tells us in 1 Corinthians 13:5, love "is not self-seeking." So seek each other's best out of freedom, and submission issues will disappear.

Boundaries and Divorce (page 248)

Remember Kelly and Scott? Kelly certainly needed some boundaries, but divorce is not a boundary in a relationship. Divorce is an end to a relationship.

- What new understanding of divorce do you have after reading the discussion on pages 248–53?

- God's solution for "I can't live that way anymore" is basically "Good! Don't live that way anymore. Do marriage my way." And God's way means acting on the behaviors suggested in the following three questions.

  — What can you do to set firm limits against evil behavior?

  — What can you do to get the love and support you need from other places?

  — What can you do to suffer long but in the right way?

- If you are considering divorce, first seriously determine what log you need to remove from your eye. Only after you have "gotten the log out" can you demand that someone else take the speck out of his.

- Review the discussion of how to repair a relationship (first printed in *Safe People* but summarized on page 252).

When will you begin this process and with what step?

Ideally, boundaries in marriage will help change and redeem the relationship. Divorce should never be the first consequence. You need to set boundaries in the context of relationship, not for the purpose of ending relationship. End your suffering and see if the boundaries you set to end your suffering can be used to bring about redemption and reconciliation as well. We have seen it happen many times in many "hopeless" situations. When one spouse finally gets true boundaries, the other one turns around. Give boundaries a chance to do their important work.

Father God and Redeemer God,

First I ask you to show me where I have misunderstood your purposes in suffering, misconstrued your definition of submission, and misused boundaries in my marriage. Show me where I am doing wrong or not doing right. Redeem my mistakes. Enable my spouse to extend forgiveness to me. And please be working in me a pattern of being loving, wise, and forgiving. As I have prayed before, I pray again: please make me more like Jesus. In his name I pray. Amen.

Embark on a
Life-Changing Journey
of Personal and Spiritual Growth

DR. HENRY CLOUD   **DR. JOHN TOWNSEND**

Dr. Henry Cloud and Dr. John Townsend have been bringing hope and healing to millions for over two decades. They have helped people everywhere discover solutions to life's most difficult personal and relational challenges. Their material provides solid, practical answers and offers guidance in the areas of *parenting, singles issues, personal growth,* and *leadership*.

Bring either Dr. Cloud or Dr. Townsend to your church or organization. They are available for:

- Seminars on a wide variety of topics
- Training for small group leaders
- Conferences
- Educational events
- Consulting with your organization

Other opportunities to experience Dr. Cloud and Dr. Townsend:

- Ultimate Leadership workshops—held in Southern California throughout the year
- Small group curriculum
- Seminars via Satellite
- Solutions Audio Club—Solutions is a weekly recorded presentation

For other resources, and for dates of seminars and workshops
by Dr. Cloud and Dr. Townsend, visit:
www.cloudtownsend.com

For other information **Call (800) 676-HOPE (4673)**

Or write to:
Cloud-Townsend Resources
18092 Sky Park South, Suite A
Irvine, CA 92614